D1015038

Other titles in the
A Retreat With... *Series:*

A RETREAT WITH PATRICK

Discovering God in All

Timothy Joyce, O.S.B.

ST. ANTHONY MESSENGER PRESS

Cincinnati, Ohio

TO MY IRISH ANCESTORS:

JAMES PATRICK and BRIDGET JOYCE,
great-grandparents, the last of our
line to die in Ireland,

JOHN and CATHERINE JOYCE,
grandparents who went on pilgrimage
to become Irish Americans,

in gratitude for all they passed on.

Scripture citations are taken from the *New Revised Standard Version Bible*, copyright ©1989 by the Division of Christian Education of the National Council of Churches of Christ in the U.S.A. and used by permission.

Excerpts from *The Confession of Saint Patrick*, edited and translated by D. R. Howlett, copyright ©1996, are used by permission of Liguori Publications.

Excerpts from Pierre Teilhard de Chardin's *The Heart of Matter*, copyright ©1980, Harcourt Brace Publishers, and *Hymn of the Universe*, copyright ©1965, HarperCollins Publishers, are used by permission of the publishers.

The excerpt from *North to the Night: A Year in the Arctic Ice*, copyright ©1998, by Alvah Simon, is used by permission of International Marine Publishing.

Cover illustration by Steve Erspamer, S.M.
Cover and book design by Mary Alfieri
Electronic format and pagination by Sandy L. Digman

ISBN 0-86716-377-1

Copyright ©2000, Timothy Joyce, O.S.B.

All rights reserved.

Published by St. Anthony Messenger Press
Printed in the U.S.A.

Contents

Introducing A Retreat With...

Twenty years ago I made a weekend retreat at a Franciscan house on the coast of New Hampshire. The retreat director's opening talk was as lively as a long-range weather forecast. He told us how completely God loves each one of us—without benefit of lively anecdotes or fresh insights.

As the friar rambled on, my inner critic kept up a *sotto voce* commentary: "I've heard all this before." "Wish he'd say something new that I could chew on." "That poor man really doesn't have much to say." Ever hungry for manna yet untasted, I devalued any experience of hearing the same old thing.

After a good night's sleep, I awoke feeling as peaceful as a traveler who has at last arrived safely home. I walked across the room toward the closet. On the way I passed the sink with its small framed mirror on the wall above. Something caught my eye like an unexpected presence. I turned, saw the reflection in the mirror and said aloud, "No wonder he loves me!"

This involuntary affirmation stunned me. What or whom had I seen in the mirror? When I looked again, it was "just me," an ordinary person with a lower-than-average reservoir of self-esteem. But I knew that in the initial vision I had seen God-in-me breaking through like a sudden sunrise.

At that moment I knew what it meant to be made in the divine image. I understood right down to my size eleven feet what it meant to be loved exactly as I was.

Only later did I connect this revelation with one granted to the Trappist monk-writer Thomas Merton. As he reports in *Conjectures of a Guilty Bystander*, while standing all unsuspecting on a street corner one day, he was overwhelmed by the "joy of being...a member of a race in which God Himself became incarnate.... There is no way of telling people that they are all walking around shining like the sun."

As an absentminded homemaker may leave a wedding ring on the kitchen windowsill, so I have often mislaid this precious conviction. But I have never forgotten that particular retreat. It persuaded me that the Spirit rushes in where it will. Not even a boring director or a judgmental retreatant can withstand the "violent wind" that "fills the entire house" where we dwell in expectation (see Acts 2:2).

So why deny ourselves any opportunity to come aside awhile and rest on holy ground? Why not withdraw from the daily web that keeps us muddled and wound? Wordsworth's complaint is ours as well: "The world is too much with us." There is no flu shot to protect us from infection by the skepticism of the media, the greed of commerce, the alienating influence of technology. We need retreats as the deer needs the running stream.

An Invitation

This book and its companions in the *A Retreat With...* series from St. Anthony Messenger Press are designed to meet that need. They are an invitation to choose as director some of the most powerful, appealing and wise mentors our faith tradition has to offer.

Our directors come from many countries, historical eras and schools of spirituality. At times they are teamed to sing in close harmony (for example, Francis de Sales, Jane de Chantal and Aelred of Rievaulx on spiritual friendship). Others are paired to kindle an illuminating fire from the friction of their differing views (such as Augustine of Hippo and Mary Magdalene on human sexuality). All have been chosen because, in their humanness and their holiness, they can help us grow in self-knowledge, discernment of God's will and maturity in the Spirit.

Inviting us into relationship with these saints and holy ones are inspired authors from today's world, women and men whose creative gifts open our windows to the Spirit's flow. As a motto for the authors of our series, we have borrowed the advice of Dom Frederick Dunne to the young Thomas Merton. Upon joining the Trappist monks, Merton wanted to sacrifice his writing activities lest they interfere with his contemplative vocation. Dom Frederick wisely advised, "Keep on writing books that make people love the spiritual life."

That is our motto. Our purpose is to foster (or strengthen) friendships between readers and retreat directors—friendships that feed the soul with wisdom, past and present. Like the scribe "trained for the kingdom of heaven," each author brings forth from his or her storeroom "what is new and what is old" (Matthew 13:52).

The Format

The pattern for each *A Retreat With...* remains the same; readers of one will be in familiar territory when they move on to the next. Each book is organized as a seven-session retreat that readers may adapt to their own schedules or to the needs of a group.

Day One begins with an anecdotal introduction called "Getting to Know Our Directors." Readers are given a telling glimpse of the guides with whom they will be sharing the retreat experience. A second section, "Placing Our Directors in Context," will enable retreatants to see the guides in their own historical, geographical, cultural and spiritual settings.

Having made the human link between seeker and guide, the authors go on to "Introducing Our Retreat Theme." This section clarifies how the guide(s) are especially suited to explore the theme and how the retreatant's spirituality can be nourished by it.

After an original "Opening Prayer" to breathe life into the day's reflection, the author, speaking with and through the mentor(s), will begin to spin out the theme. While focusing on the guide(s)' own words and experience, the author may also draw on Scripture, tradition, literature, art, music, psychology or contemporary events to illuminate the path.

Each day's session is followed by reflection questions designed to challenge, affirm and guide the reader in integrating the theme into daily life. A "Closing Prayer" brings the session full circle and provides a spark of inspiration for the reader to harbor until the next session.

Days Two through Six begin with "Coming Together in the Spirit" and follow a format similar to Day One. Day Seven weaves the entire retreat together, encourages a continuation of the mentoring relationship and concludes with "Deepening Your Acquaintance," an envoi to live the theme by God's grace, the director(s)' guidance and the retreatant's discernment. A closing section of Resources serves as a larder from which readers may draw enriching books, videos, cassettes and films.

We hope readers will experience at least one of those memorable "No wonder God loves me!" moments. And we hope that they will have "talked back" to the mentors, as good friends are wont to do.

A case in point: There was once a famous preacher who always drew a capacity crowd to the cathedral. Whenever he spoke, an eccentric old woman sat in the front pew directly beneath the pulpit. She took every opportunity to mumble complaints and contradictions— just loud enough for the preacher to catch the drift that he was not as wonderful as he was reputed to be. Others seated down front glowered at the woman and tried to shush her. But she went right on needling the preacher to her heart's content.

When the old woman died, the congregation was astounded at the depth and sincerity of the preacher's grief. Asked why he was so bereft, he responded, "Now who will help me to grow?"

All of our mentors in *A Retreat With...* are worthy guides. Yet none would seek retreatants who simply said, "Where you lead, I will follow. You're the expert." In truth, our directors provide only half the retreat's content. Readers themselves will generate the other half.

As general editor for the retreat series, I pray that readers will, by their questions, comments, doubts and decision-making, fertilize the seeds our mentors have planted.

And may the Spirit of God rush in to give the growth.

Gloria Hutchinson
Series Editor
Conversion of Saint Paul, 1995

Getting to Know Our Director

Hail glorious Saint Patrick, dear Saint of our Isle,
On us thy poor children bestow a sweet smile,
And now thou art high in the mansions above,
On Erin's green valleys look down in thy love.
                    —Traditional hymn to Saint Patrick

Patrick, principal patron of the Irish, must surely be one of the best known of all saints. In many countries, his feast day is annually celebrated with huge festivals, colorful parades and well-attended liturgical celebrations. Schoolchildren learn the doctrine of the Holy Trinity in the story of Patrick's use of the image of the shamrock. Many are named Patrick or Patricia in his honor. I myself took the name of Patrick when choosing a patron saint at the time of my Confirmation.

And, yet, how many people really know much about this fifth-century Christian Celt? Most of the well-known stories about Patrick come from the popular lives and songs based on early medieval sources, the earliest written some two hundred years after his death. These tales recount Patrick's missionary journeys throughout Ireland, when he is said to have converted and baptized thousands of people. In these writings, Patrick is portrayed as a miracle worker, as one who confronted and overpowered the druids, a teacher who used the shamrock, a shaman who chased the snakes out of Ireland, a saintly man who fasted for forty days and forty nights on the holy mountain. One story tells of an episode in which Patrick lit a fire in an Easter celebration on the hill of Slane and thus openly challenged the king who, on the nearby hill of Tara, was lighting the only fire permitted in the land during the native spring feast of Bealtaine. These tales connect Patrick closely with the Church in Gaul where they claim he was educated and ordained. They tell us it was Patrick himself who determined the primacy of the Irish Church at Armagh.

This is the Patrick about whom many Irish schoolchildren learned in the Maynooth Penny Catechism. These sources, as well as later chronicles and lives, contain some authentic facts and historical truths. But they also need to be treated with some caution. First, they contain some contradictions of facts, names, places, times and significance of events. Second, we have to understand these stories in the way that people of Patrick's time would have written and comprehended lives of the saints. "Hagiography" was not just history. It was common practice to portray the life of a holy person in ways that resembled the lives of Jesus and the saints, thus building up the case for the acceptance of holiness in this particular person. Similarities and parallels were important. So Patrick appeared as a great miracle worker and seer. He was like Moses, Elijah and Christ himself in his forty-day fast on the mountain. Like Moses, he encountered God in a burning bush. These events might actually have happened, but ancient hagiography wasn't concerned with whether they really happened or not. The stories were meant to portray what was in the heart of the saint. The third problem in interpreting these sources is that the reader questions whether the stories are being used in part for propaganda. They portray Patrick as a bishop sent by Rome to build up the Church in the fashion prevalent in Rome. From this perspective, Patrick appears to conflict with the native customs and "pagan" traditions of the Irish. He then is seen as a stern patriarch

bringing law and order to the "tribal and wild natives"—
intent on obliterating their heritage and culture.

Still, many of these stories are helpful in telling the
story of Patrick. But they need to be subordinated to a
more solidly based source for the facts of his life. We are
blessed with two such documents written by Patrick
himself, both of which are universally accepted by
scholars and are authenticated in many manuscripts.
These documents were not widely known until a
standard edition of them was produced forty years ago.
The first is a short autobiography that is called the
Confession of Saint Patrick. The second is a letter Patrick
wrote to Coroticus, a British tribal chief, concerning the
abduction of some Irish youths into slavery in Britain.

These two documents provide a gold mine of
information about the real Patrick. And the Patrick that
they reveal is a beautiful man indeed. It is true that they
describe the inner man more than his external
circumstances, and we would certainly like to know a lot
more about his life and times. But, nevertheless, they
provide us with an intimate picture of at least certain
aspects of this remarkable person.

Drawing on story, legend and fact, what do we know
about Saint Patrick? He was probably born in Roman
Britain about the year 415.[1] The place of his birth must
have been close to the Irish Sea where pirates and
brigands from that not too distant Irish isle were
patrolling the waters. His home might have been in Wales
or, more likely, north of Wales in Cumbria around modern
Carlisle. The Britain of the time was, of course, Celtic,
though it had become part of the Roman Empire. The
Angles and Saxons were not yet on the scene and there
was no England. Patrick's father, an owner of a small
estate, was a decurion, a member of the Roman provincial
governing class. He was also a deacon of the Church.

Patrick's grandfather was a priest. While this would indicate a religious household, Patrick tells that, as a boy, and like most youths around him at the time, he was neglectful of religion. At the age of fourteen or fifteen, he committed some sin which bothered him all his life. Then in the year 430-431, Irish raiders came into the district of his father's farm and carried him off, with many others, into slavery into Ireland. He was then sixteen years old.

Patrick spent the next six years in slavery, tending flocks, often alone for long periods of time. Experiencing a profound interior conversion, he discovered God was very close to him in his distress. In time he heard a voice in a dream telling him to leave. He walked across Ireland, boarded a ship going east and landed, with the crew, in Britain or possibly France. Eventually he found his way back to his parents' home where he resumed his life. It was not long, however, before he heeded the call to seek ordination as a priest. Then, in another dream he heard a call to return to Ireland. And so he began the years of his active ministry among the Irish people. This was not an easy and totally carefree time, and he once again was taken into captivity. Worse than the physical sufferings were the accusations and criticism he received from other churchmen of the time. His *Confession* is an attempt, in his old age, to justify his life before God and the Church.

Patrick's "Letter to Coroticus" is an impassioned document protesting the taking of Irish youth into slavery in Britain. It is quite an extraordinary piece of history as he appears to be the first European to raise his voice in protest against the institution of slavery. This writing, as well as the *Confession*, gives us an intimate insight into the heart and mind of Patrick.

In his writing, Patrick protests that he is a rude and uneducated man. He was mindful of the fact that he had been abducted in his youth before completing formal studies in school. He was criticized by jealous ecclesiastics for not being "up to his job." Perhaps Patrick really believed this to be true. Perhaps he did not consider their criticism as worth challenging. It is unfortunate, however, that readers over the centuries took him literally and spoke of his writings as being simplistic and crude. But modern scholarship has shown the contrary to be true. His writings are much more sophisticated than previously understood by many readers.

The *Confession of Saint Patrick* is divided into five short books or chapters. It has been discovered that they reflect both the first five books of the Bible (the Torah) and the five collections of sayings in the Gospel of Matthew.[2] The first chapter corresponds to Genesis and tells us of Patrick's beginnings. Then comes Patrick's Exodus, the story of his escape from captivity across the sea. The third chapter mirrors Leviticus, telling of Patrick's problems with ecclesiastical authorities and detailing his own canonical status. The fourth chapter, like the Book of Numbers, relates Patrick's ministry and work of evangelization. Finally, Patrick's Deuteronomy tells of his own preparation for death. The complete work is suffused with sacred Scripture, often just woven into the text. And, finally, it has been discovered that the style is highly complex consisting of concentric and parallel constructions.[3] No, this is not a casually written book. And the "Letter to Coroticus" is no less a finely crafted piece of literature.

In the end we get a picture of our director that is quite satisfying. Far from being a distant and imperious bishop coming in with great power to sway the multitudes, his own *Confession* shows Patrick to be a very human and very humble man. He struggles, faces failure, deals with criticism and rejection. He is a man of great faith in the presence of an intimate Trinitarian God. He is a committed Christian who is passionately devoted to Christ and the gospel. He is aware of his sinfulness, weaknesses and inadequacies. Patrick is convinced that the goodness of God is to be found in all people and throughout the created world. He is a dreamer and visionary, open to the God of his imagination. He is a missionary with a sense of purpose and vision. He loves the poor and the outcast. He embraces the people that had enslaved him as a youth.

Patrick died around the year 493, but we do not know exactly where. The place of his captivity in youth seems to have been in western Ireland in County Mayo near the sea.[4] We are not sure if he returned there as bishop or traversed much of Ireland, settling, as tradition says, in Armagh in northern Ireland.[5] Though a tombstone in Downpatrick claims to mark his burial place, we really do not know where he died or where he was buried. He probably died as a simple man completely unaware of his noble contribution to the tradition of Christianity in Ireland. "Hail glorious Saint Patrick..." his spiritual sons and daughters have cried for fifteen hundred years.

Placing Our Director in Context

Patrick lived in the fifth century, a time of rapid change and transition. In many ways we might say that those times of turbulence and uncertainty were not unlike our own. The Roman Empire was beginning to break up, and Europe was about to enter the so-called Dark Ages. Rome fell to barbarian invaders in 410. Within ten years of that time, the Roman forces began to leave Britain to return to Rome to defend positions back home. Life, once so orderly and predictable under Roman domination, now became chaotic and uncertain. Patrick entered the world of that time.

Ireland itself, of course, unlike Britain, had never come under Roman control as the planned invasion of Ireland never was achieved.[6] With Britain becoming more vulnerable, Irish war bands began to patrol the British coast taking booty and slaves. The inner condition of Ireland at the time remains largely unknown. The writings of Patrick are the only historical documents we have from Ireland for the entire fifth century. It is generally believed that Ireland, still a rural society, was experiencing some decay as old ways were breaking down in an isolated and regressive culture.[7]

The British Church of Patrick's time was also intimately connected with the Roman Empire. Missionaries from the continent followed the development of Roman towns, travelling over the system of good Roman roads. This was an urban Church with bishops establishing their centers in these Roman towns. The great ecumenical councils, beginning with that of Nicea in 325, doctrinally solidified a developing and common faith throughout this Church. Britain, and the Celtic Church, became a cause of concern to the churches of Rome and Gaul for its following of the heresy of Pelagianism. This heresy, named after the British monk Pelagius, emphasized the human ability to attain perfection through asceticism. It also seemed to deny original sin and downplayed our need of grace for becoming holy.

As Ireland had not come under the Roman Empire, it was for the most part unnoticed and untended by the developing Church. There were some Irish Christians, mostly on the eastern and southeastern coast. Many of these were probably British slaves who had been taken into captivity by the Irish. There is a record of a Bishop Palladius being sent to Ireland before Patrick. But the mission of Patrick was unique. There had been, up to this time, no other organized or concerted missionary effort to convert any pagan peoples beyond the confines of the Roman Empire. Patrick's efforts to do this, in fact, were criticized as being a useless project. His call had come to him in a personal vision. Although it must have been validated by some ecclesiastical superior, it was a cause of jealousy and ridicule on the part of other churchmen. The more we see Patrick in the setting of his time, the more we must admire his courage, vision and faith. But we also see that his path brought him pain and suffering. Acclaimed as a great hero in ensuing centuries, he himself felt nothing of the sort in his own time.

Patrick, then, is an intensely human person and not a plaster saint to admire from afar. He offers us a Christian vision of life honed out of his own experience and trials. He offers us a challenge to live our own Christian life today in changing and turbulent times. He comforts us when we are criticized and ridiculed. He gives to us the Celtic vision of the intimate presence of God in creation, in the Church, in people and in Scripture. He is a model for us, giving us an example to follow as we struggle to live authentically our own Christian lives in our own difficult times.

Notes

[1] While Patrick's dates are contested, I am accepting the scholarship of Liam De Paor in his work, *Saint Patrick's World: The Christian Culture of Ireland's Apostolic Age* (Notre Dame, Ind.: University of Notre Dame Press, 1993). See, particularly, "Ireland in the Fifth Century," pp. 23 ff., and "St. Patrick's Writings," pp. 88 ff.

[2] See D.R. Howlett's fine introduction, pp. 33-39, in his translation and edition of *The Confession of Saint Patrick* (Liguori, Mo.: Triumph, 1996).

[3] For a detailed analysis of Patrick's literary finesse, see Máire B. de Paor's *Patrick, The Pilgrim Apostle of Ireland: St. Patrick's Confession and Epistle* (Dublin: Veritas Publications, 1998). See the Introduction, "Patrick the Writer," pp. 9-21.

[4] Another story, coming from later sources, shows him to be a captive in northern Ireland.

[5] One tradition has Patrick returning to Ireland at Saul, near Downpatrick in County Down.

[6] There is some evidence of the existence of some Roman fortifications in Ireland, but the Roman presence was never extensive nor sufficient to really influence the local culture.

[7] Liam De Paor, pp. 23 ff.

DAY ONE

Discovering God in All

Introducing Our Retreat Theme

The theme of our retreat is discovering God in all. What we are seeking is the real, fully alive and present God. Sometimes Christians, in attempting to live a good and sincere life, ask themselves the question, "What would Jesus do?" if he were here in these circumstances. I suggest that the question should be "What could Jesus be saying here and now?" What does the living Christ himself do and want us to do in our everyday lives?

The mystery of the Christ, God made flesh, has both tantalized and confused Christians for two millennia. Historically, we have found it difficult to keep a balanced understanding. Some heresies have denied the humanity of Christ. Jesus, from this point of view, is God in a human appearance, like angels who, in biblical stories, took a human form to communicate with earthly beings. This Christ is worshipped and adored, but perhaps at times pushed too far away from us, elevated from, and outside of, his creation. Other intermediaries, such as saints, then must fill his role as mediator and human representative.

But Christ is God made flesh who is to be embraced as our way to the Father. He is the head of the Church and of every Christian community. He is the leader—the center—of every Christian gathering. No other human being can take his unique place.

However, the divinity of this Christ can be forgotten or underemphasized as well. He becomes so like us that he is a buddy, a friend, an exemplar, merely one of many humans in history who helps us to find our way to God. The result is the loss of the cosmic, transcendent and mysterious realities of Christ.

The Christ who is human and divine, intimate, cosmic, transcendent and mysterious is the Christ, I believe, that Patrick discovered, whom Patrick loved, whom Patrick followed and shared with others in a work of passion and service. Patrick had been taught about Christ in his home. But it was in his own experiences that he discovered this intimate and loving Christ. Open to see God's plan in his own life's journey and open to the people and culture in which he unexpectedly found himself, Patrick sought and gradually found a Christ that was in all and everything, a Christ whom he could have hardly imagined in his youth.

In this retreat we let Patrick guide us in our own search for God. We will look at some themes that emerge from his writings, his *Confession* and his "Letter to Coroticus." The medieval lives of Patrick will not be entirely neglected either in our attempt to understand the life and teachings of this holy man. Finally we will also draw upon the so-called "Breastplate of Saint Patrick," a wonderful prayer that sums up so much of Celtic spirituality. Scholars who have examined the language do not believe Patrick wrote this personally; it is usually dated some two to three centuries after his death. Perhaps it was preserved in a largely oral culture and later updated and recorded. Perhaps it was adapted from some ancient prayer of Patrick. Or perhaps it was not his at all. In any event, the content of the prayer is thoroughly consistent with the writings of Patrick and helps us to place his thought and piety in a wonderfully prayerful expression of praise.

We look at all these ancient writings in the context of what we know of the Celtic Christian Church, and how we have come to understand and imagine Patrick's message in today's Church and world. So a stanza from the breastplate will be the opening and closing prayer of each day and offer us our day's theme.

Opening Prayer

> For my shield this day I call:
> A mighty power:
> The Holy Trinity!
> Affirming threeness,
> Confessing Oneness,
> In the making of all
> Through love....

O holy Three-in-One God, I arise today through the power of your love and goodness. You are all that is and can be found in all that exists, and I hope to find myself in you. I arise today mindful of your creating touch in my whole being and in the being of this good world in which you have placed me. I arise today, knowing that Christ walks with me before you, Father, with the power of your Spirit. May your holy name be praised as I seek to know myself better, to understand better this world in which I live and thus come to understand the Christ through whom, with whom and in whom all of my world holds together.

RETREAT SESSION ONE
You Are Not Alone

Truly, if you have the Celtic spirit, you know that Patrick still lives. He is here with us now. Try to imagine this presence. The typical holy card picture may not really help. Rather, imagine some wise and gentle elderly person you have known. Patrick is a wise and well-proven senior. He has been tested in life, come through adversity, has emerged as a kind, tolerant and loving person. He looks upon you as a younger brother or sister whom he loves and wants to help. He wants to share his story with you.

His viewpoint now is from eternity. He remembers his time on this earth, and he can still experience it. He also knows the events which followed his time here, the successes and failures of Christianity in Ireland and throughout the world since then. He knows the stories of the millions who have sought meaning in their lives, as he did, by being open to life's experiences. Let him speak to you now and share his story.

"It is good to have these days to share some thoughts with you. Come and take the time to slow down and be with me in prayer and reflection. I will be praying for you and with you as you retreat this week.

"Consider, my friends, have you ever experienced a significant and painful loss in your life? I believe that this is part of the life experience of most, if not all, people. For some it is the death of someone they really love. For others it is the loss of a job or a place of position. Perhaps you have been betrayed by a friend or suffered some form of injustice triggered by jealousy. Some people have been scarred by their experiences in war or by abuse sustained while either a child or adult. As for me, my world fell apart right before my sixteenth birthday. My carefree and secure world was shattered when I was kidnapped and taken captive into a foreign land.

"I Patrick, 'a sinner,' very rustic, and the least of all the faithful, and very contemptible in the estimation of most people, was captured. I was then almost sixteen years of age. I was indeed ignorant of the true God, and I was taken in captivity to Ireland with so many thousands of people...because we turned away from God and we did not keep watch over his precepts.[1]

"My home was in Britain, then a province of the Roman Empire. The years before my birth were generally peaceful and prosperous, though uncertainty grew as the Roman authorities began to be more concerned with threatening circumstances back in Rome. I came from a good, solid family and was blessed with love, good care and physical well-being. We had a rather good-sized farm which my father administered. He was a minor official in the provincial government and was also a deacon of the Church. His father was a priest and also lived in our area. So I had good religious training, a solid foundation in Christian belief and practice. I was educated in our local school of grammar. I had friends and we enjoyed doing things together, such as fishing and collecting firewood in the hills. At this time in my adolescent life, there was also a girl who held considerable attraction for me. I suppose I had it all and didn't realize it. I certainly was not a serious lad. Church, religion, education, work and responsibility were all tedious parts of my life for which I compensated by having much fun and engaging in some rebellion.

"Then, one day, as a few of us boys were on our way home from school and were walking in a wooded area, we were ambushed and taken captive. I was filled with a fear such as I had never known before. With bonds on hands and feet and a gag in my mouth, I was thrown into a cart where I began to tremble and cry. Soon we were on a boat and in chains. When we had crossed the sea and arrived at the land, which I came to know as Ireland, I was blindfolded, separated from the others. All I wanted to do was somehow undo the past few hours and be back in my own safe home. 'O, God,' I prayed, 'Do not punish me for my evil ways. I will mend my life and be more serious if only you restore me to my home and good parents.'

"Before long the journey was over and I was released into the hands of a farmer someplace near the sea. I had no idea where I was. I was frightened, I was sick and in a state of near delirium. Reality set in slowly. I spent the next six years as a slave for my new owner, tending sheep and doing menial tasks. As I grew to young manhood, I was kept in a condition of servility, struggling with hunger, cold and near-nakedness. The physical pain and discomfort were bad. But the mental torment was worse. I believed I was being duly punished for the sins of my youth and that this was to be my lot for life. I was terribly lonely, abandoned and scared.

"I began to recite the prayers I had learned as a boy. Being alone for hours on my own, I would simply repeat them over and over. And then that very loneliness became a school of solitude and inner silence. I was forced to be with myself and look at myself in a way that I would never have chosen. I contemplated my soul and was frightened by what I saw. There was no escape, no place to run. And then, the miracle happened. By staying with my poor self and slowly coming to a certain acceptance, I reached a place of deep peace. I was overwhelmed by an encompassing and protective presence that I could only call God and recognize as the Triune God of my Christian upbringing. I felt like the prodigal son unaccountably loved by God who was

Father. I felt closely allied with the Christ who suffered
and with whom I was now suffering. I experienced the
comfort and touch and inner breath of the Spirit that
glowed within me. I cried for happiness even while
lamenting my predicament as slave.

"There the Lord opened my heart to an awareness of my
unbelief so that, perhaps, I might at last remember my sins, and
that I might turn with all my heart to the Lord my God, who
turned his gaze on my lowliness and had mercy on my youth
and ignorance and kept watch over me before I knew him...and
he protected me and comforted me as a father comforts a son.[2]

"God in his goodness, I realize now, had been
preparing me for this conversion. I not only had to face
myself but also was completely open to the might, power
and beauty of God's created world. I learned from the
sheep I tended, the birds that greeted me each day, the
winds and the sea that surrounded me, and even the rain
that fell so frequently. Sunrises and sunsets, the monthly
resurrection of the new moon, the nobility of trees, the
wild red deer, the elk and other animals were all
revelations of God's wonderful universe, even the wolves
and foxes who threatened the sheep! All of creation
proclaimed to me the glory of this God whom I was
learning to recognize.

"And then there were the people—my captors—
simple hardworking people not very different from those
I had left behind in Britain. These were a people who
lived close to the earth and who were intimate with the
divine, the world of the spirit, which they apprehended in
everything. They had a keen sense of the presence of the
other world and of all who had gone before them. They
never seemed alone. And I learned from them.

"I could have become bitter during this experience,
hardened and forever concerned only for myself. I could
have been consumed with my anger, fear and self-pity. I

look back with wonder and realize that none of these
things happened—God's grace and love proved to be
stronger than my own smallness and my pitiful
resistance.

"The miracle of that experience is that I found I was
not alone, that my God was intimately close to me, that I
was cared for and loved. My time of captivity turned out
to be a time of proving and growth. Because I had learned
to attune my exterior senses to the presence of God in
nature and in the people, my interior senses also
developed. I became more sensitive to the reality of the
spirit world and of the Holy Spirit stirring within me.
When I was ready, a voice in my heart said that I must
leave and that a boat awaited me on the eastern shore.
My time of captivity had come to an end. After a long
journey, I was able happily to return to my parents' home.

"You are well aware, I am sure, that I eventually did
return to Ireland. The Spirit continued to guide me, to
speak to me. After some restless pondering, I decided to
pursue a vocation to the priesthood. Because my formal
education had been interrupted years before, this was not
to be an easy undertaking. After my ordination to the
priesthood, my knowledge, interest in and love of the
Irish came to the attention of the ecclesiastical authorities.
When a voice summoned me back to Ireland, I was
chosen to be a bishop to bring the gospel to these people
at the edge of the (then) known world. The years after
that brought much satisfaction as I traveled among the
people of Ireland, speaking of the love of the triune God.
I suffered hardships and isolation at various times. I was
once again taken into captivity and put into chains. I was
an object of scorn, jealousy and suspicion. And the worst
part of it was that it did not come from the 'pagan'
peoples of Ireland. It came from my ecclesiastical peers
who derided me for my incompetence, my lack of

learning and my simple and inept ways of evangelizing. One former friend revealed a story of my youth, an old sinful experience that has always shamed me, thus casting disgrace upon me. I was discouraged and often tempted to give up what seemed to be a foolhardy adventure.

"Despite all that I endured, that intimate presence of God which I had found in captivity never left me completely. 'You are not alone, Patrick,' I would hear, 'you are not alone.' Unworthy and inept as I was, God had chosen me and was with me. I did not understand why, and sometimes I wished it were otherwise. The years in Ireland brought struggle and setbacks. But the grace of the Lord flowed through my work and many people embraced the Christian faith. I can only give praise and thanks to a God who never forsook me, even when many around me did.

"*Therefore I give unwearied thanks to my God, who kept me faithful in the day of my trial, so that today I may confidently offer in sacrifice to him my life as a living host to Christ my Lord, who has saved me from all my troubles.*[3]

"I am sure that you, too, have experienced some large crisis or setback in your life. I know I was not unique in my life's struggle. I offer you my story on this first day of retreat so that you may reflect on your own journey and realize how you are never really abandoned, that you are never alone, that there always is for you, as for me, a God present and ever loving to accompany you on your way."

For Reflection

- *Like Patrick, when have you experienced a great loss that became a source of growth and soil for conversion? How were you able to emerge from this loss with greater love and faith? How do you deal with the scars that need healing so new life may come forth?*

- *In our own time we have witnessed the tragic and horrific experiences of many people. Terry Anderson was a hostage in Beirut for almost seven years, often in solitary confinement. He came forth, due to his faith, as a stronger and more compassionate person. Nelson Mandela spent twenty-seven years in a South African prison but emerged with seemingly little bitterness or anger. How do you think you would have handled a similar experience? What are you doing now that can prepare you for such an experience?*

- *It is part of the human predicament to experience loneliness. How do you recognize your own need for silence and solitude? What forms of discipline and asceticism do you practice to help you grow in self-knowledge?*

- *Patrick's conversion was due in part to his acute attunement to the created world around him. His exterior senses became aware and appreciative of the natural universe as revealing God's presence, love and goodness. How does nature, in both its beauty and its awesome power, reveal to you the triune God who has "made all through love"?*

- *The sensory openness to all of God's creation further helped Patrick to open his interior senses of awareness and perception both of the world of the Spirit and of the closeness of Christ, Mary, the angels and saints. In what ways do you open your soul to the spiritual world?*

Closing Prayer

For my shield this day I call:
A mighty power:
The Holy Trinity!
Affirming Threeness,
Confessing Oneness
In the making of all
Through love...

Blessed and all holy Three-in-One God, I confess my belief in your intimate and all involving presence in my life. I acknowledge you have made all through love. All the earth, all the universe, every human being, and every human experience I have lived has been full of your intimate and guiding love. Help me, with Patrick as a guide, to believe more strongly in that presence and to live my life in more open awareness of the gifted world around me and within me. Help me in my loneliness to know you are near. Help me to hear your voice that reminds me that I am never alone. To you be honor and glory. Amen.

Notes

[1] *Confession*, I, v. 1. All quotations are from the translation of Máire B. dePaor, pp. 221-265.

[2] *Confession*, Part I, v. 2.

[3] *Confession*, Part III, v. 34.

Day Two
My Christ Is With You

Coming Together in the Spirit

On this second day of our retreat, we come upon
Patrick who has been deep in reverie, reflecting on his
mission to the Irish. He knows that, over the years, many
have wondered why the Irish embraced Christianity so
quickly and peacefully. For Patrick, this is not so
mysterious. He believes that the person of Christ was
irresistible to these Celts. To these nature-loving people
who had, at times, worshipped the sun, Patrick gave
them the image of Jesus Christ, the true Sun who shines
forever and who gives light to all who live in darkness.

The Irish were among those Celtic peoples whose
culture had enjoyed a first great age of prominence in the
five centuries before the coming of Christ. These were a
passionate and warring people who loved heroes. Tales of
pre-Christian Ireland come together in the epic story of
"The Cattle Raid of Cooley" which centers on the heroic
figure of Cuchulain. This mighty warrior is a precursor of
the age of chivalry as he often represented his entire clan
in one-on-one battles. He personally represents the best of
the people. Significantly, from a Christian point of view,
his last battle occurred while he was wounded and tied to
a tree for support.

In the times following their defeat under Julius
Caesar in Gaul, the Celts had gone into a period of

eclipse.[1] Patrick helped them to develop a second great era of Celtic culture, but this time illumined by the figure of Christ. Today Patrick wants to share some of his love of Christ with us.

Defining Our Thematic Context

Yesterday Patrick related the story of his conversion. He explained how he had found the intimacy of a triune God surrounding and embracing him. We reflected on the circumstances of our own lives when we seem to be overwhelmed by loneliness or feelings of abandonment. Can we begin to appreciate that we are never really alone? Do we feel the closeness of a loving God?

The wonder of the Christian revelation is the Incarnation. God has become one of us. God is to be found in the human. We need not search and find God only in the unseen, in the things of the spirit. God has become flesh. He has loved with us, worked with us and laughed with us. Like ourselves, he has hungered and thirsted and been fatigued. He has been tempted and discouraged and confused like us. He has loved banquets and celebrations and good friends like us. He has suffered and felt pain like us. He has died as all of us will.

Patrick found his particular comfort and meaning in the caring presence of a God who walked with him and shared his sufferings and attempts to live a good life. Today let us listen to Patrick relate some of his insights about the Christ with us.

Opening Prayer

> For my shield this day I call:
> Christ's power in his coming
> and in his baptizing,
> Christ's power in his dying
> on the cross, his arising
> from the tomb, his ascending;
> Christ's power in his coming
> for judgment and ending.

Lord God, heavenly Father, long ago you created the universe by speaking your Word through whom all things were made. You continued to be with us in all creation through the power of that Word and your Spirit. But your love went even further in sharing that Word with us in the flesh of Jesus Christ, your Son, who became human with us and for us as our brother. Continue to speak that Word in our midst and, through the power of your Spirit, may we come to know and love that same Jesus Christ, your Son, who lives and reigns with you and the Spirit as one God forever and ever. Amen.

RETREAT SESSION TWO
Christ's Power Upholds Me

"Today, my friend, I want to talk to you about the Christ in my life and yours. But, first, I must say something about being human. When we look into the face of an innocent child, or see a youngster playing and lost in happiness and wonder, tears often come to our eyes for we see the beauty of being human. Our days as adults are not always like that (nor, unfortunately, are they for some children). But there is more to human life than innocence, happiness and wonder. Sorrow and pain also are part of life. There were times, especially when I was in captivity, and again in the weariness and discouragement of later life, that I doubted the value of my life and wasn't sure I wanted to live much longer. I am sure that most people have experienced that on some days. But on most days I was able to rebound and find value and meaning in my life. And, now with the power of hindsight, I can say all of my life was worth living.

"I must not hide 'The Gift of God' which has been lavished on us 'in the land of my captivity,' because then I earnestly sought him, and there I found him, and he kept me from all iniquities, this is my belief, 'because of his indwelling Spirit,' who 'has worked' in me up to this day.[2]

"To be human is a great gift and sometimes a great challenge. Being human is a vocation and carries the responsibility of developing our bodies, feeding our souls and opening our spirits to the Spirit of God. It is also to accept our place in the universe as finite, limited and very vulnerable creatures. I learned early that I was a very insecure person and I felt very threatened at times. But time and experience showed me that all people are insecure. We all find ourselves as little people in a big world, trying to make our mark or at least to find some significance and meaning in who we are and in what we do. This often means we try to be 'number one' in some area of life, to excel and show that we really are somebody. That usually works for a while, especially when we are young and have lots of energy and drive.

"Eventually, however, a Copernican revolution is demanded. In my time people thought the earth was the center of the universe—everything revolved around us. Later in history, it came as a shock to many that the earth is not the center of the solar system nor of the cosmos. In

the same way, as individuals, we have to learn that we
are just one of many billion persons passing through this
world. There is a center, indeed. That center is not us, it is
God. Surrendering and accepting our total dependence on
this God, and interdependence on each other, is one of
life's most profound lessons.

"That is where Christ comes in. I believe that in
finding Christ in my life, I have discovered what being
human is all about. Christ is the way we learn to be
human. That is what happened to me and what happened
to the Irish. In my fears and sorrow in captivity, I
remembered the stories of Christ I had learned as a boy. I
began to be comforted in the knowledge that, although he
was God, he became totally human like me.

"I was lonely. I was fearful. I felt abandoned. I was
discouraged and depressed. Then, I came to realize that
Christ, too, experienced all of these feelings. Christ was
suffering with me again. My life was not useless and
empty. I did not really comprehend this way of living and
loving. But I knew that being with Christ in what he
experienced brought me meaning. A God that would
identify with us and embrace even suffering shook me in
my own feelings of desolation.

"Christianity was accepted in Ireland in a very short
time with little opposition. Though I was an instrument in
this phenomenon, a power beyond me was at work. The
Irish were a naturally religious people, and their Celtic
background included embracing the reality of the other
world, the sacredness of creation and all reality as well as
the preciousness of relationships. For them the Christian
doctrines of the Holy Trinity, of the sacramental view of
creation and of the communion of saints were all
corroborating mysteries which seemed natural to them.
But it was especially the mystery of the Incarnation, God
made flesh in Jesus Christ, that captured their hearts and

brought them new meaning.

"The Celts had always loved, admired and even worshipped heroes. They were, in many ways, a heroic people themselves. Shortly before my time, they had been repulsed in Gaul, Spain and Britain by the Romans, many fleeing to Ireland and other marginal areas of the known world. Now they were no longer a prominent people. Christ came to them as superhero, one filled with the passion of a warrior, the wisdom of a Druid, the storytelling of a bard, the strength of a king. But he was also a human being who understood their rejection, their suffering, their darkness. They understood well that he was not a hero to acclaim from afar. He was close, near to them, intimate in their lives. He was a brother. He was the sweet son of his mother Mary whom he shared with them as well. They knew that he walked among them, lived with them, embraced all of their lives' journey. In more recent centuries, Irish Christians, who have suffered so much, have honored this intimate Christ, whom they recognized as suffering with them, in the image and the title of the Sacred Heart of Jesus.

"There are some Christians who can accept Christ and his humanity in theory. But in reality they accept only his divinity. So they back Christ away from them and elevate him far above themselves, make him a source of gifts and favors, and try to placate him through prayers and works. The challenge for all today is to adore this Christ as God and yet accept his humanity seriously, to believe in faith that he is really our one mediator bridging heaven and earth. The Celtic mind had already been endowed with a sense of the closeness of the divine and the other world. Perhaps that mind can help us today in coming to know and love Christ better and more intimately.

"We know that the Christ, the Son of the Father and the giver of the Spirit, is close to all of us. All of creation was made through Christ the Word and that creation reveals him to us daily. He is the head of the body which is the Church, the people of God, and there, too, we recognize him as teacher, priest and prophet. We recognize him in the least of his people—the poor, the hungry, the sorrowful, the oppressed and marginalized. It is little wonder, then, that hospitality was so important to the Celtic Christians and has remained important to their descendants.

"But Christians have two special sources of the life of Christ that express his closeness to us and enable us to keep his memory and teachings alive. These two sources are the sacraments and the sacred Scriptures."

Christ in the Sacraments

"It was my joy as bishop and evangelizer to bring the sacraments to the Irish people. They were ready to accept the significance of a God who could be intimately present to them through material things. Because they were a people of poetry and symbol, the Irish enthusiastically embraced the Church's sacramental system. Many Christians today continue to respond to the human need for ritual and to the power of symbol by embracing the sacraments. Those who have become estranged from the Church for one reason or another usually admit to missing the sacraments. They are such a powerful source of Christ's life for people.

"*There in Ireland I choose to spend my life until I die, if the Lord should grant that to me, because I am very much God's debtor, who has granted me such grace, that a multitude through me should be reborn to God, and afterwards be confirmed, and that clergy everywhere should be ordained for them. It is indeed our duty to fish well and diligently...that a copious multitude and throng should be taken for God.*[3]

"When I baptized I knew it was Christ who washed

and purified the new Christians so that they become part of his Body. Now they could conform their lives into his pattern of death and resurrection. In Confirmation it was the Christ who gave them his Spirit. When we convened for the Eucharist, it was the Christ who became present in the assembly. They could now say 'we are the Body of Christ.' It was the Christ who spoke to them in the Scriptures. It was the Christ who was present in me as the priest leading them in the offering of their lives with Christ to the Father. It is the Christ whom the Father gave back to them in Holy Communion. And it continues to be the life of Christ that all Christians relive and the mysteries of Christ that they touch when they live the liturgical feasts of Christmas, Easter, Pentecost and all the lesser feasts throughout the year. It is through the sacraments that we are truly immersed in Christ's power in his coming and in his baptizing, Christ's power in his dying on the cross, his arising from the tomb, his ascending, and it is Christ's power in his coming for judgment and returning all to the Father that experience in the sacraments."

Christ in the Scriptures

"Coming to know and love Christ also calls us to be his disciples, to embrace his teaching, attitudes and concerns for our world. The memory of what I had learned from the Bible in my youth helped me get through my captivity. When I returned home, I turned to the Scriptures to 'put on the mind of Jesus Christ' as Saint Paul counsels us to do.[4] In the Old Testament stories I acquired a deeper understanding of myself. Like the chosen people, we are called by God but regularly forget that call and wander off on our own way. The prophets call us back to our baptismal covenant. We cannot understand Christ without knowing the Old Testament.

He is integral to it. He brings it to fulfillment as he becomes the first one to be fully human in responding to God's call. He prayed and preached the Hebrew Scriptures. Following the example of Christ, the Celtic monks, from the beginning, embraced the psalms as their 'day in and day out' prayer. The psalms, which Jesus prayed, are the greatest school of prayer.

"In the New Testament, the four evangelists each gave me a particular perspective in my understanding of Jesus. Saint Paul gave me rich reflections on the meaning of Christian life. All of the Scriptures are gifts of God and open us up to the mind of Christ. Saint Jerome, who lived shortly before me, was wont to say that to be ignorant of the Scriptures is to be ignorant of Christ. I think he was right.

"So, my dear retreatant, you can see that we have many ways to come to know the Christ, God's gift to us as human beings. The Irish of old appreciated that gift. Certainly, they lived in different times than you do. Their main concern was for survival, for basic necessities of food and warmth, and for some meaning in a world that was still very mysterious and, at times, threatening to them. You have different struggles and problems. Life is a lot more complicated for you even with all the scientific and technological benefits available today which were unknown to the ancients. Because people live longer, you are often concerned with the health and well-being of your elderly parents and relatives. You struggle to find your own place and to help your children to find their place in a competitive and confusing world. And there is so much loneliness and isolation. People live with so many fears and feelings of being overwhelmed by uncontrollable forces.

"Is not our intimacy with the Christ, the God who knows us fully and experientially in the human flesh of

Jesus Christ, desperately needed today? Is not knowing Christ better and entering into a personal relationship with him a way to find meaning and fulfillment in our lives? The times require a deepening of our relationship with him, a more intensive and internalized life with him. Today, for my shield, I take up the power of Christ to guide and protect me."

For Reflection

- *In what ways are you aware of not yet fully accepting your humanity? In what ways do you deny your mortality, your vulnerability, your lack of control, your embodiedness and all that this entails? How might Christ help you in your endeavor?*

- *In what ways do you take Christ's humanity seriously as an opening for you to relate to him in a personal way and yet accept that he is God?*

- *What is your understanding of sacrament? How does Patrick help you to see the sacraments as a personal encounter with Jesus Christ? When, if ever, does the humanity of the Church, priest and other Christians get in the way of your meeting Christ? How might you deepen your understanding of sacrament?*

- *How is the Bible a personal encounter with Jesus Christ for you?*

- *What is missing in your own life that would allow you to be a more committed disciple of Jesus Christ? How might Patrick help you do something about that?*

Closing Prayer

> For my shield this day I call:
> Christ's power in his coming
> and in his baptizing,
> Christ's power in his dying
> on the cross, his arising
> from the tomb, his ascending;
> Christ's power in his coming
> for judgment and ending.

O great and all loving God, I praise and thank you for the gift of your Son. Through him, the Word of God, you created all that is and this good world reflects that Word to us. But, still more lovingly, you established a new creation in the humanity of Jesus Christ, the Word made flesh. O that I might come to know him more deeply, love him more intensely, and live his life to the fullest in my own human existence. I ask the gift of your Spirit to bring your Christ alive in me every day. Amen.

Notes

[1] The defeat of the Celtic tribes, united under Vercingetorix, in Gaul, 52 B.C., was a climactic turning back of the Celts. They withdrew to the northwestern perimeters of Europe and never again were to be a major force in history.

[2] *Confession*, Part III, v. 33.

[3] *Confession*, Part IV, v. 38-40.

[4] See 1 Corinthians 2:16 and Romans 11:34.

Day Three
Surrounded by a Cloud of Witnesses

Coming Together in the Spirit

In today's world we consider time to be a valuable asset. We measure it accurately, and much of what we do is determined according to the clock. Digital watches have given us a new vision of time. Time and speed in athletic races can be measured within hundreds of seconds, and computers can even measure a nanosecond! While all of this modern technology has some scientific merit, we are no longer as conscious of how it changes the way we see life, the succession of events, the separation of now and then.

The ancients had a different way of conceiving time. The Celts, in particular, thought there was lots of time and it wasn't particularly important. Place was very important—where something took place or where you would locate something. But time was quite a secondary thing. It was a common occurrence to talk of things in the past as though they just happened today. A vivid example would be the stories about the life of the second patron of Ireland, Saint Bridget.[1]

Bridget has always been much loved by the Irish, who have venerated her as "Mary of the Gaels." The straw cross of Bridget guards many a home from evil. Her

feast day, February 1, subsumed much of the old
midwinter Celtic festival of Imbolc. There is a legend
which tells of her working at the inn where Mary and
Joseph stopped and were given directions to a cave where
they could bed down. The story goes on to say that
Bridget left the inn, followed Mary and Joseph and served
as midwife to the birth of Jesus. Later, so the story goes,
she was the one who helped Mary and Joseph find Jesus
in the temple when he was lost at the age of twelve.
Fanciful? Yes, but time is irrelevant in the mythical
picture of Bridget. The storyteller is interested in telling
us something else, more to do with presence and
relationships than with time and facts.

The scientific and humanly constructed ways of
dealing with the physical world will not be enough in our
contemplation of spiritual realities. We will have to
expand our mind's way of conceiving time. Patrick
knows this from experience and will share insight with us
today.

Defining Our Thematic Context

Patrick, as our director, has spoken to us of our
transformation and conversion to living in the conscious
presence of God. Then he spoke to us of Jesus Christ, our
mediator with God. This Christ, we realize, is accessible
to us through physical realities. He is touched and
experienced in people. His power, emanating from the
mysteries of his own life, flows into our life, like an
energy, through the sensual experiences that we call
sacraments. His word is heard, spoken and savored in the
Scriptures. We truly do touch the Christ in these sources
of life.

God also is present to us through His Spirit, who

reminds us of, and intensifies, everything that Jesus has done and taught. There are sources of the presence of God that are invisible and purely spiritual. However, most of these are also mediated presences through other created beings. We are not alone in this universe. Whenever we celebrate Mass, we hear proclaimed in the Preface the following words—"and now with all the choirs of angels and saints we together sing: holy, holy, holy." The angels and saints are present to us through the Holy Spirit. The communion of saints is a doctrine particularly reassuring to us in our loneliness. Today, Patrick explores the significance of this aspect of spirituality.

Opening Prayer

> For my shield this day I call:
> strong power of the seraphim,
> with angels obeying,
> and archangels attending,
> in the glorious company
> of the holy and risen ones,
> in the prayers of the ancestors,
> in visions prophetic,
> and commands apostolic,
> in the annals of witness,
> in virginal innocence,
> in the deeds of steadfast people.

God, we come before you today, eager to continue this retreat journey with you and with Patrick. As we travel our life journey on earth surrounded by a cloud of witnesses of angels and saints, we ask the grace to have the spiritual eyes to perceive their presence more acutely, to travel more consciously in their presence. Send forth your Spirit to awaken our spiritual senses to be aware of

the gifts and reality of this spiritual world. We ask this
through Christ our Lord.

RETREAT SESSION THREE

Communion of Saints, Angels and Pilgrims

"I hope we are comfortable with each other by now
for I am going to share something with you that may
strike you as rather strange. The unfolding of much of my
adult life as a Christian, priest and a missionary came
about through the prompting of inner voices. Some
people today might be amused by anyone making such a
claim. In my time it was not that extraordinary. Or, at
least, I didn't think it was extraordinary. I certainly wasn't
particularly sensitive in my youth to voices from the
other world. But my time in captivity, a time of solitude
and soul-searching, opened my heart to the voices that I
truly believe are constantly echoing in the souls of many
people.

"As the years passed I found some peace and serenity
in the knowledge of the protection of the Holy Three-in-
One who were walking with me in this new land. Then I
heard a voice in my head and heart saying I should
prepare to leave Ireland. At first I thought it was more my
own wish and desire speaking. But it kept recurring. I
began to accept the real possibility, with a sense of joy
and excitement, that my time of captivity would be
ended. Then I heard a different message telling me to
leave and start walking east where I would find a ship to
take me back to Britain.

"*One night in a dream I heard a voice saying to me, 'It is well that you are fasting, soon you will go to your own country.' And again after a short time I heard the answer saying to me: 'Look your ship is ready.'*²

"My master had learned to trust me over the years, and I was left alone at night with no fetters of any kind. So, one night when all was quiet and still, I simply departed and started the long trek across the land to the Irish Sea. I was able to find a ship where the sailors, after a brief period of turning me away, agreed to take me with them. And so I left, never to return—or so I thought. I wandered with them for a while, first on sea and then on land, and was eventually taken captive once again. And, once again, I heard a voice cautioning patience, predicting I would be free in two months. And, on the sixtieth day, I was able to escape both from my captors and the sailors and finally to return to my parents' home. I was grateful to a God who had tried me and helped me to grow and now had brought me home.

"Let me share just one more of my voices with you. This one was more of an inner vision. One night I imaged a man coming from Ireland. His name was Victoricius, and I saw that he was carrying many letters. He gave me one letter containing the 'Voice of the Irish.' It addressed me as 'holy boy' and requested me to come back and walk among them again. This was my call to return to Ireland, this time as priest and ultimately as bishop, to bring the good news of Jesus Christ to the people among whom I formerly was held captive.

"*As I was reading the beginning of the letter aloud I imagined I heard, at the moment, the voice of those very people who lived beside the Wood of Fochoill, which is near the western sea, and thus they cried out, as if from one mouth, 'We request you, holy boy, that you come and walk once more among us.' And I was truly cut to the heart, and I could read no further.*[3]

"I can tell you that the Celts, even in pagan times, always believed that the other world and this world were separated only by a very thin membrane. They believed that, at certain times and places ('thin times' and 'thin places') even that veil would disappear, and the ancestors and other spiritual beings would appear among them. As a Celtic Christian I had known that this applied to angels and saints, as well as to my own personal forebears. They were all, really, quite close. And so I found in my captivity, as I would find often in life, that I was never really alone."

The Presence of Angels

"Do you believe in angels? I note that they have been very popular in the recent piety of the western world. Unfortunately, they often seem to be trivialized into sweet and harmless human-like presences. The Bible has a very different image of angels. They are God's messengers, they are the very voice of God. They often comfort and assist human beings. But, sometimes, they challenge them as well. Right from the beginning we see them, in the Book of Genesis, guarding Eden after Adam and Eve are exiled from the paradisal land. In the ensuing story, they guide the chosen people through the desert.

"Some angels, in individual human guises, intervene in the lives of individuals—visiting Abraham, wrestling with Jacob, guiding Tobias. Angels announce the birth of Christ and direct the shepherds to the crib. Angels at the tomb direct the confused disciples to seek the risen Lord. So we cannot deny the existence of angels. In the Celtic tradition, shrines were built on the top of mountains and other high places in honor of the great warrior angel, Michael, who was particularly revered.

"Angels are, indeed, real. Some of you might have to

transcend the shortcomings of your scientific age which accepts as true and real only what can be proved by physical sciences in order to accept this deeper plane of reality. There is another kind of reality and another kind of knowledge which belongs to a spiritual world that is just as real as the material world. The Celtic tradition did not pit one against the other, did not make one higher than the other, but accepted and lived with both aspects of one reality. That became my personal experience. I hope it is yours, too. God continues to be with you and communicates with you in many ways."

The Presence of Saints

"But it is not only the angels who are present with us. All the saints are alive in God and alive with us. The doctrine of the communion of saints proclaims the unity of all human beings who have loved and followed God— whether they be on earth or in heaven. Many Christians pray to the saints and call on them to intercede for us here on earth. The saints not only pray *for* us but also pray *with* us as they share our journey. In my time we believed that Mary and the Apostles were the special holy humans who shared our journey. Mary was pictured, not so much as a Queen on high and remote from us, but rather as a lovely barefooted peasant girl who walked among the villages and stopped to talk with people and share their joys and sorrows.

"The saints were 'soul-friends'—fellow humans with whom we talked in order to discern our own path. Saint Paul, Apostle to the gentiles, was my particularly special soul friend. I believed he empathized with me as a stranger in a foreign land, trying to share the Good News, and at times suffering rejection and physical hardship. Saint Paul's great love for Christ, expressed in his epistles, brought me very close to this holy man.

"Christians have always been baptized with the name of some saint whom they call their patron saint. But these saints are much more than patrons. They are unique friends, who walk with and guide their namesakes. I feel particularly close to all those who, over the centuries, have been named Patrick or Patricia. A name is more than a label. It is an identity. I share my identity with other Patricks and Patricias. It is always a matter of sadness for me to observe people name their children after some fashionable person of the day, some television personality or celebrity. I feel sorry for the child who has no real saint as a soul friend. If you know someone like that, you might suggest he or she take some saint as a special friend whether he or she bears the name or not. It is also possible to find other saints as soul friends, those who shared a similar vocation or experienced a similar difficulty in their own life's journey."

The Presence of Our Ancestors

"The Celts always used the title 'saint' very freely. There were no official saints in the early centuries of the Church; saints were acclaimed by the people. I was never officially canonized myself. Saint Malachy in the twelfth century was the first officially canonized Irish saint, but there were many saints before him. The word *saint* in the early Church, as used in Paul's letters, referred to any good Christian. In this light I would like to suggest that you look upon your own deceased parents, grandparents, ancestors and fellow journeyers in family, community or life also as saints! They, too, still walk with you, continue to be present in your life. Perhaps, at certain times, you have recognized such a presence. A certain occasion, such as an anniversary, often brings the deceased person so close we sense that they are present. In your scientific and critical mind you may immediately dismiss that as just the imagination. But could it be otherwise?

"It is my perception that many modern folk find it difficult to really apprehend the spiritual world because you live with so much noise. Some silence and solitude are needed in order to allow the spiritual senses to develop. It was during those long, dark and very silent nights that I began to be at home with my own soul and to recognize the movements within it. That time was painful at first but truly necessary. Perhaps that is why, in your times, so many people are turning to various forms of meditation. I suggest you look at Christian centering prayer, meditation or any similar practice that helps you to quiet the outer senses and open up the inner world.

"Also, do not be concerned if you find yourself apprehensive and fearful about death. It is only natural. Some say that we come into the world alone and we leave alone. I do not believe that. We were tended by the angels and saints at our birth, and they will be there at our death, and that includes our beloved ancestors. If you begin now to consciously become aware of their presence in your daily living, you will certainly know you are not alone when you arrive at the place of your resurrection.

"To sum up this difficult topic, my dear friend, I want to reiterate the reality of the spiritual world. I think children know there is a spiritual world. Their minds and hearts are open. Perhaps they still bear some memory of the God from whom they came and of the angels and saints who welcomed them at their birth. But in the extreme self-consciousness of adolescence, people tend to lose that awareness completely. In the uncertainty and insecurity of growing up, a young man or woman looks to others to affirm what is right and good and acceptable in life. Succeeding and making a mark in the world beyond the confines of family and village also means fitting into a larger society and following its ways.

"The world that you live in today is a secular one. God is a sideline to be believed in if that is useful. Belief in spirits, angels, living saints and holy ancestors is not something you are likely to talk about at a party. But, as you seek to grow as a spiritual person, you may come once again to know the reality of other spiritual beings who are all around you and who want to help and accompany you. So, this day, we call on all of them to be our shield in life, a shield against the dark powers that assault our faith, our love, our struggles to be good and compassionate people. We call upon them to help us believe more strongly and to love with ever greater commitment and perseverance.

For Reflection

- *What do you think of the inner voices that Patrick describes? Have you ever had such an experience?*

- *What sense of angelic powers do you have? How do you image angels in your mind? How do these images correspond with biblical images?*

- *What saints do you turn to as soul friends? Are you acquainted with those (whether canonized saints or ancestors) for whom you have been named?*

- *Wakes and funerals were always important events for the Celts, and were always to be celebrated in a communal and joyful fashion. Why do you think that was so? How would you like your funeral to be celebrated? You might choose to plan it now.*

- *Are you afraid to face your death? How are you preparing for it by developing a sense of the living closeness of angels and saints in your life?*

Closing Prayer

For my shield this day I call:
strong power of the seraphim,
with angels obeying,
and archangels attending,
in the glorious company
of the holy and risen ones,
in the prayers of the ancestors,
in visions prophetic,
and commands apostolic,
in the annals of witness,
in virginal innocence,
in the deeds of steadfast people.

Almighty and all-beautiful God, your holiness and goodness are reflected in all of your creation. Today we praise you for those you have created as pure spirits to serve you and be of service to all the living on earth. We thank you for all the holy men and women of former times who have gone before us as a crowd of heavenly witnesses and helpers. We are grateful for our own relatives and ancestors whose spirit still lives in us, with us and around us. May they all give glory to your holy name, even as they guide and protect us. May we, with them, reflect your creative and benevolent hand.

Notes

[1] Bridget was abbess of a dual monastery of men and women in Kildare. The dates for her life are generally accepted to be about 452-524.

[2] *Confession*, Part II, v. 8.

[3] *Confession*, Part II, v. 23.

DAY FOUR

The Holiness of
the Created World

Coming Together in the Spirit

Our growing interest in the care of the environment, a greater awareness of its limitations and our own relationship to the material world, as well as an increased knowledge of the ecology of the world that unites us all—these are all a sign of the Holy Spirit at work among us. For too long all of us, Christians included, have misused God's created world and selfishly ignored what our usage and practices have meant to those in other parts of our planet, as well as to future generations. Our religion has, too often, been compartmentalized into only that which happens in church. Only matters of the mind have been considered the subject of our faith, to the detriment of feelings, the body and the material world with which we interact. False splits between what God has first made in creation and what he has redeemed by grace have led some to denigrate the natural world as somehow unimportant, if not even bad and sinful.

While some people today look to Native American or other spiritualities, many of us are looking to our own Christian tradition to find a more holistic look at creation. To begin with, we find it in the Bible. The Book of Psalms particularly gives us a prayerful attitude to creation. And

the Canticle of the Three Youths, found in the Book of
Daniel, is especially evocative:

> Bless the Lord, all you works of the Lord: sing praise
> to him and highly exalt him forever.
> Bless the Lord, sun and moon.... Bless the Lord, stars
> of heaven....
> Bless the Lord, all rain and dew.... Bless the Lord, all
> you winds....
> Bless the Lord, mountains and hills.... Bless the
> Lord, all that grows in the ground.
> Bless the Lord, all birds of the air.... Bless the Lord,
> all wild animals and cattle....
> Bless the Lord, all people on earth....
> Bless the Lord, all you spirits and souls of the just.[1]

Many of the medieval mystics, such as Meister Eckhart,
Julian of Norwich and Hildegard of Bingen, continued
this biblical tradition and are popular today partly
because of their mystical view of nature. Thus we read in
Eckhart that he believed if he spent enough time with the
tiniest creature, even a caterpillar, he would never have to
prepare a sermon, so full of God is every creature.

In our own time, writers such as Pierre Teilhard de
Chardin, S.J., and Thomas Berry call us to a theological
understanding of the cosmos which honors and
appreciates nature and praises the holiness of matter.
Chardin, in his "Hymn to Matter," wrote in a mystic and
daring voice:

> I bless you matter, and you I acclaim...as you
> reveal yourself to me today, in your totality and
> your true nature.... Blessed be you, impenetrable
> matter.... You who batter us and then dress our
> wounds, you who resist us and yield to us, you
> who wreck and build, you who shackle and
> liberate, the sap of our souls, the hands of God,
> the flesh of Christ; it is you, matter, that I bless...[2]

Is there something in the Celtic tradition, specifically in the life and words of Patrick, that can help us in this new appreciation?

Defining Our Thematic Context

The fourth stanza of the "Breastplate of Saint Patrick," with its invocation of the natural world to give us God's protection, is one of the most remarkable expressions in Christian history to give voice to the holiness of creation. Later, in the thirteenth century, Francis of Assisi would pen something similar in his "Canticle of the Creatures" in which he embraced the sun as brother, the moon as sister and all other natural elements, including Brother Ass, as his siblings.

We consider this spirituality of creation on this fourth day of our retreat. We began our retreat on the first day with a sense of God's imminent presence. Then we saw how this is made real and visible in Christ. Yesterday we looked at the ways that God's grace and life is brought to us through his creatures who are spirits or who have gone forth from this world to live the new creation in God's presence. Today's theme is a look at another way in which God is present to us—this time, in every part of the created, material universe. Patrick will share this wonderful aspect of the Celtic Christian tradition and ask us to attune our senses to see and behold the divine, the holy, in the everyday manifestations of this world.

Opening Prayer

For my shield this day I call:
Heaven's might,

Sun's brightness,
Moon's whiteness,
Fire's glory,
Lightning's swiftness,
Wind's wildness,
Ocean's depth,
Earth's solidity,
Rock's immobility.

All-powerful God, who has made all through love, and expressed your own Triune nature in the wonderful variety of this universe, we praise and thank you for this world of ours. We acknowledge the goodness of all you have made and ask forgiveness for our despoiling of its beauty and our preventing its availability to all your children. Help us, in our meditation, today, to be more aware of the grandeur of all you have created.

Retreat Session Four

The Earth Is the Lord's and the Fullness Thereof

"I feel confident that you appreciate the beauty of the natural world and often find inspiration from it. But do you connect this spiritual experience with that of your Christian faith and revelation? I observe that, for some, there is a real split between the two. It wasn't always so. A number of Christian preachers over the ages have spoken of the two books that God has written—one of creation, the second of Scripture. God reveals himself and his plan of salvation in both. And it is Christ who is at the heart of both. It was through the Word that all things were made. It is in the Word made flesh that the supernatural world of grace is revealed.

"As Christians, are to take the world very seriously, we are to reverence all of creation and material reality, we are to know that the flesh is holy. Christianity is a religion of the Incarnation. The material world and, specifically, human flesh has been taken on by God. All of the cosmos, already made good in creation, has been lifted high in Christ. Yet, sadly, there have been recurring heresies that have denied the goodness of creation, have tried to bypass the world and matter in search of the spirit, and have even looked upon matter, particularly the body, as bad. The Celtic tradition to which I was heir was quite different.

"Both my native Britain and the Ireland of the fifth century had received the heritage of a tribal and communal people, close to the land and to all the natural elements. They respected and reverenced all of creation. Christianity brought this to a sharper focus in the teaching of the Word made flesh. It likewise helped the people to cope better with their fears of the natural world and see a benevolent God revealed in creation. It was no longer necessary to worship and placate nature itself.

"It was the power of nature itself that helped me in my turning to the triune God. In the loneliness and deprivation of my slavery years, I began to read God's book of creation more attentively. The sun, moon, sea, wind and rain, wild animals as well as my flock of sheep who taught me how to trust God as my Shepherd—all began to share something of God and my own place in God's universe. They helped me to rediscover Jesus Christ as I began to recall, from the Scriptures, that he was a fellow human being who also learned from nature and constantly taught with stories and parables of the natural world.

"After I had come to Ireland, I was herding flocks daily, and many times a day I was praying. More and more the love of God and fear of him came to me, and my faith was being increased, and the Spirit was being moved, so that in one day I would say as many as a hundred prayers, and at night nearly the same, even while I was staying in the woods and on the mountain; and before daybreak I was roused up to prayer, in snow, in frost, in rain; and I felt no ill-effects from it, nor was there any sluggishness in me....[3]

"Let me share some of the things that God's natural world taught me."

Trees That Teach

"Trees were very holy in the Celtic pre-Christian religion. Groves of trees, particularly oaks, were the main places where people gathered to worship. Trees are important in salvation history, too. Genesis begins with a story of the tree in paradise. The Christ is lifted high on a tree to gather all things to himself. The Bible closes with a tree of life in the new paradise.

"Yes, trees are significant teachers to us. I would often sit and stare at a large tree and focus on its beauty and strength. I would think of how stable and rooted, how persevering this tree was. I realized that the old tree in front of me was there before my birth and would be there after my death. That helped me to see my own place in this world—a passing guest of the God of creation. I marveled at the tree losing its leaves every autumn. How gently it seemed to surrender, to let go, to even die. It knew how to remain fallow and bear the winds, ice and snow of winter. And it always brought forth new life in the spring.

"Yes, I could learn from a tree. And I could try to be

more like a tree. The very first psalm says that those
whose delight is in the law of the Lord are like trees
planted by flowing water, who yield their fruit in due
season and who prosper in all they do. When you are not
sure of how you fit into God's plan, I suggest you sit
down in silence before a tree and try to learn its lesson."

The Wind and Sea

"The sea, as well as the wind, have also been constant
voices of God for people. The ever restless, ever moving
sea has a rhythm and beauty of its own. It reverberates in
music and prayer. The wind, too, has marked the way we
learn to pray and sing and echoes in much of our music.
Life-giving water cleans and purifies and yet can also
destroy. Winds comfort and cool, but also can overturn
the weak and poorly rooted. There is so much to learn
from and with nature. I think the beauty of much of Irish
music and poetry is indebted to its echoing the sea and
the wind."

The Sun and Moon

"The sun is a particular source of revelation of God to
us. As a giver of life and warmth, the sun has often been
worshipped. It was the object of much of Celtic worship,
as it was for the Germanic tribes of our time. I wanted to
help the Irish understand that Jesus Christ was the true
sun who was life, light and truth. The sun itself is not
God even while conveying the life that comes from God.
Perhaps Christians, however, have lost the sense of the
sacredness of the sun and all of creation. Let me tell you
of one incident in my life that, once again, may seem
strange to the modern mind. It happened shortly after I
had escaped from Ireland and was still with the boatmen
on land. We had been travelling for twenty-eight days

through deserted countryside. Because I had helped them find food, and, thus, they considered me a miracle-worker, I began to feel rather important. Look what I had done! But we were again hungry and without food, and I couldn't do a thing to help. I was beginning to doubt whether God had really been with me and was on the brink of a new despair.

"Like the Israelites in the desert, I even began to look back to those years in slavery as more secure and alluring. That night my pride and all my doubts and fears were shaken in a vision of the power of darkness in Satan who was tempting me to give up faith and to cease counseling my fellow travelers to persevere in patience and hope. I was terrified by a power that seemed to oppress, suffocate and annihilate me. I felt my body being violently attacked and then pinned down with a giant rock so that I could not move. Then, for some reason I could not understand (it had to be the Holy Spirit praying within me), I called on Elijah the prophet. I wrote about it later in this way:

"Lo, the splendor of his sun (helios) *fell on me, and immediately freed me of all oppressiveness, and I believe that I was sustained by Christ the Lord, and that His Spirit was even then crying out on my behalf.*[4]

"The risen Christ, the Sun of justice, came to me as the sun. And, I believe, the Christ, released in the cosmos by his Resurrection, does come to us through the sun and in so many other material ways.

"In the era following my lifetime, Christians knew the power of Christ in creation. They prayed to the sun as the eye of God, the eye of the King of the living, as the face of the God of life. Many Christians would climb a hill or mountain on Easter morning and watch for the sun to dance, revealing the resurrected Christ as the 'Lord of the Dance.' Poems and songs proclaimed that wondrous event. The scientific minds of your time might look upon this as fancy. But what might the eyes of faith really be able to see?

"The moon, too, preaches in its own way of the presence of God. The new moon, in particular, has been the subject of many prayers. When Christians of my time looked upon the tender crescent of the new moon, they immediately saw a sign of new life, rebirth, resurrection. The old moon had once again died, but a new one was reborn. The Christ was being made evident in the night sky. Their thoughts then turned to those who had died since the last new moon, in the previous twenty-nine days. No formal prayer is needed. Just look at the moon, remember the dead and lift them up to the risen Lord, reflected in this sight."

The Dark Side of Nature

"There is also, to be sure, the dark side of nature of which the Celtic peoples were most aware. We will consider the dark side of reality on the sixth day of our retreat. For today, we simply acknowledge that it exists. We need protection from the forces of nature just as we need an appreciation of its awesome beauty."

On Holy Ground

"What I am suggesting to you is that you integrate your love and appreciation of nature into your spiritual life, into your Christian life. Like Moses before the burning bush, we must take off our shoes and know that we are on holy ground. God appeared to Moses through a visible created thing, a bush. Unlike most of the appearances of God to us in nature, the divine presence in that case broke through the veil that ordinarily hides that presence. The bush burned but was not consumed. We have to see the presence of God in the material creation with the eyes of faith. We have to know that we are always on holy ground. Can you think of your house, your garden, your own property as holy ground? Do you recognize the voice of God in the branch of a tree blowing in the wind? Do not the daffodils of spring tell you that our God is a God of new life? From there, try to bring that attitude everywhere you go, and be more and more aware of the holiness of all creation.

"It has been said that if a person is out of touch with creation, he or she will be out of touch with God. That is a danger for you today. So many take for granted the availability of the food that they eat daily without being aware of what the earth has so freely given. Light, heat, clothing, furniture and all the commodities that we use come, ultimately, from the earth. They have been fashioned for us by the handiwork of many intermediary people whose own spirit has been embedded in these objects. Everything connects us to God and to each other. The material world is holy because God has made it and sustains it by his providential and loving presence. It is holy because it is the common ground for all of us to use, the common thread that unites all of us as brothers and sisters."

Sins Against Creation

"One sin against God's creation manifests itself in the accumulative and wasteful spirit that is rampant in the consumerism of the day. Many people have too much. They think that more and more possessions will give them meaning, identity and happiness. Theirs is an anti-materialistic spirit. The true materialist respects matter, reverences it, does not abuse or misuse it, is careful of how it is preserved. The believer does not look at the world as a scientist might, that is, as an object to be studied, dissected and controlled. The believer relates to the world as a fellow creature and respects its place in the divine economy. That is quite a difference. The world is a subject and not just an object. It is our dignity, as human beings, to give it voice and consciousness and to help redeem it. As the blessed Apostle, Paul, wrote:

> [C]reation waits with eager longing for the revealing of the children of God; for the creation was subjected to futility, not of its own will but by the will who subjected it, in hope that the creation itself will be set free from its bondage to decay and will obtain the freedom of the glory of the children of God.... [T]he whole creation has been groaning in labor pains until now; and not only the creation, but we ourselves, who have the first fruits of the Spirit, groan inwardly while we await for adoption, the redemption of our bodies.[5]

"Another sin that manifests itself in our abuse of creation is our misuse of the human body, the temple of the Holy Spirit. It is wrong to deny the holiness of the body, the goodness of the flesh and the great gift of human sexuality. A heresy has recurrently erupted in Christianity which debases material things, considers them evil and denounces the human body and sexuality as particularly evil. That is a non-Incarnational, spiritualistic approach that fears matter and the body and is, ultimately, embarrassed by a God made flesh. True care and reverence for the body are called for in our tradition. But we must remember that we are responsible for how we use the body just as we are responsible for all of creation. We must care for the body and use properly the gift of sexuality as part of the authentic Christian life.

"To develop a more wholesome attitude toward creation, read God's book of creation. The practice of *lectio divina*, prayerful meditation on God's word, can be done with both the Bible and creation. So, pray and reflect on a flower, a tree, the wind or the sea. Stay with it for a while, and let it touch you and let it reveal God's word to you. Write a poem or a prayer to celebrate that word and that lesson to allow it to abide within you.

A second practice is to foster a simplicity of life-style. That may be the real asceticism called for today. Reject consumerism and avoid shopping and buying just for recreation. Reverence what you have by not over-accumulating more than you really need. Be aware of how you use or abuse what you have. Develop a desire to share the goods of creation with all people, especially those in need of the basic materials of food, housing and clothing."

For Reflection

- *Where, in nature, are you most at home? How do you feel in that place? What does God say to you there?*

- *Is it a problem for you to find the same God in both Church and in nature? Is there a way you can integrate them more intimately and holistically?*

- *Have you had any experiences when the veil that separates this world and the other seemed to be dissolved? When was God right there in the "burning bush" of your own experience?*

- *In the context of today's culture, what might foster a deeper, more meaningful relationship between Christian worship and the natural world? How might you help others to experience this relationship?*

- *In what ways do you foster or reject consumerism? How do*

*you recognize the holiness of your own body and sexuality?
How do your behavior and attitudes relate to those of
contemporary society?*

Closing Prayer

For my shield this day I call:
Heaven's might,
Sun's brightness,
Moon's whiteness,
Fire's glory,
Lightning's swiftness,
Wind's wildness,
Ocean's depth,
Earth's solidity,
Rock's immobility.

God, who has made all things in love and sustains
them in love, we praise and thank you for the wonders of
this world. Forgive us for our misuse of creation, of all
the material world, and of our human bodies. Open our
hearts to hear your voice in all of creation and help us to
work with that creation to serve and praise you always.

Notes

[1] Daniel 3:29-68.

[2] Pierre Teilhard de Chardin, *Hymn of the Universe* (New York:
Harper and Row, 1965), pp. 64 ff.

[3] *Confession*, Part II, v. 16.

[4] *Confession*, Part II, v. 20. There is a play on words here in the Latin
text. Patrick calls upon Elijah as "Helia, Helia!" and is greeted by
the sun (*helios*).

[5] Romans 8:19-23.

DAY FIVE

On a Journey With God

Coming Together in the Spirit

Patrick was a pilgrim to Ireland. After his time, many Irish men and women traveled in the opposite direction, from Ireland to Britain and the continent. Columcille went to Iona in Scotland; Columban established monasteries in France, Austria, Switzerland and Italy. Perhaps the best known Irish pilgrim in early Christian times was Brendan the Navigator (486-578). Brendan was a Kerryman who made journeys to Wales and Scotland. But the stories of his sea journeys are especially notable. Adventures with the elements, with sea monsters and with various local peoples make for exciting reading. The record of his journeys, called the *Navigatio*, was a favorite piece of literature throughout the Middle Ages. Of course, he was also supposed to have sailed to Nova Scotia and thereby "discovered America" in the sixth century.

Pilgrimage has once again become popular in Europe. As once before, people are traversing the countryside to go to holy shrines and historical sites. They often go by foot, some across England from Canterbury to Iona, some across the Pyrenees to Compostella, others over the Alps and south to Rome. Although the practice is somewhat less evident in the Americas, places such as Guadalupe in Mexico and the shrines of Mary and Joseph in the French Province of Quebec in Canada have always attracted spiritual travelers.

Human beings need a sense of place. They need to belong to a particular people and to a particular place. But the human spirit also needs to seek, to journey, to reach out beyond the familiar and static. There is both comfort and discomfort in the tension of these two needs. And there is a highly spiritual dimension to both.

Defining Our Thematic Context

Patrick has been leading us into a heightened sense of the immanent presence of God. We are gradually being led to understand how Christ has broken all barriers for us and brought the divine, the transcendent, the Other, intimately close to us. Our director has already shared some of his love and appreciation of this Christ. He has opened our hearts and souls to the presence of angels and saints, God's intermediaries, and to the presence of God in the natural, created world of the cosmos.

Today, Patrick speaks of two particular aspects of finding and touching God's presence—the aspects of pilgrimage and place. At first, these may seem to be contradictory; but they are related and may be better understood as two sides of one coin. As we each travel on our life's journey, let us probe what pilgrimage might mean to us today. As we each live in a particular time and place, so let us consider what that might mean for our spiritual life.

Opening Prayer

This day I call to me:
God's strength to direct me,

God's power to sustain me,
God's wisdom to guide me,
God's vision to light me,
God's ear to my hearing,
God's word to my speaking,
God's hand to uphold me,
God's pathway before me,
God's shield to protect me,
God's legions to save me.

Almighty God, as you once called Abraham and Sarah to set forth from their secure and comfortable home to begin life anew, help me to heed your call to stay on life's journey. As you sent Mary, Joseph and Jesus into Egypt to escape the wrath of Herod, help me to undertake the journey that is required to flee from any destructive forces in my own life. And help me to appreciate the good all around me, in the people in my life and the gifts you give me every day to encourage me. Praise to you for all your gifts, given in the Spirit, through Christ Our Lord. Amen.

RETREAT SESSION FIVE
To Be a Pilgrim, to Be in Place

"I give thanks to God who has strengthened me in all things so that he did not impede my setting out on the journey on which I had decided, nor also from the task which I had learned from Christ my Lord, and my faith was approved before God and people.[1]

"I have been honored to be called 'Apostle of Ireland.' That certainly makes me feel close to my soul-friend,

Saint Paul, the apostle to the gentiles. But I would never have thought of myself in those words. I considered myself, rather, a pilgrim, one sent on a journey to a new land, a land which, at that time, was thought to be at the very ends of the earth. As a matter of fact, I was always an alien in Ireland. As such, I had no rights there and was not protected by the Brehon laws which governed those tribal peoples. I was always in a very precarious position and when arrested and taken captive, I really felt akin to Saint Paul!"

On Pilgrimage

"Perhaps you have had the experience of being an alien dwelling, at least temporarily, in a foreign land. That can prove to be difficult and uncomfortable at times, though it also widens our understanding of humanity and broadens our cultural education. Living in another country for a while makes us see that what we take for granted in our own upbringing as 'normal' is, in fact, quite dependent on our culture. Our own perceptions and customs are not the criteria by which we should judge others. There is more than one way to see things, and to do things. Unfortunately, many travelers today expect (and demand) to find their own culture everywhere they go. International companies and consumerism have brought about a dreadful sameness to many places around the earth. There is, also, an insidious, if hidden, imperialism lying in the demand that everyone else should be and act like ourselves.

"Learning to be a pilgrim can provide a new spiritual experience. To become a pilgrim means to make a journey. The way along the route is just as important as the destination. On my own journeys in Ireland I was blessed to have many Irish Christians share the journey along the way. I found that being a pilgrim calls on you to share stories, to share food and drink and to share laughs as well as some inconveniences. It was always a communal endeavor—as it has been for many others over the years. People share history, tradition and the connectedness with those who have gone before them (and who accompany them on this journey). They touch the places where others have journeyed and thus touch their times as well. On a pilgrimage, you journey together and then celebrate, at some shrine or place, an event or happening of the past that you can now claim for yourselves. Today many people visit ancient monastic sites in Ireland, such as Glendalough, not just to study history but to touch the monastic center of their own souls, to learn from Saint Kevin[2] and others how to seek God above all things in their own lives.

"I have to admit that it may happen that, after you have been traveling for a while, it can all become tiresome. You want to return to your own country, your own bed, your own routine. That is understandable. But I think that such an experience is really part of being a pilgrim, too. It helps you to understand how a displaced person might feel. And that could be a spiritual gift. We shouldn't run away from it. When we get out of our own comfortable groove for a while, then we can better appreciate that all people are only passing through this world and that here on earth one has no abiding city. We must not build too secure a nest.

"We must learn how to accept God's hospitality and not think we have to be in control and be the host ourselves. What we possess is to be shared and passed on to others when we finish our journey here. Once having withdrawn from the cultural ways of your own milieu, which include materialism and consumerism, you may find that you want to find a way to remain on the margins and live in some countercultural way."

Pilgrimage as Prayer of the Body

"There is still another good benefit of pilgrimage. It is a prayer of the body. You have to move, to walk, sometimes to climb. And that is good for our spiritual life, to say nothing of our physical well-being too! Religion can become much too cerebral when faith is confined to doctrine—simply something to believe, to know, to memorize. Authentic spirituality is how we live out what we profess. The body must be involved. Works of caring and works of justice are some ways to show the faith in action. Pilgrimage, along with some ascetical ways of praying such as keeping vigil and fasting, are also prayer in action.

"In my life's experience, there was much that was physical. I had to walk the hills and woodlands of Ireland to bring the gospel to the people. I was put in chains. I fasted. During Lent I would follow the example of Christ and go apart for a while. One year, I spent forty days in prayer and fasting on top of a mountain.[3] Since that time, pilgrims have continued to climb that mountain, now called Croagh Patrick in western Ireland, often walking barefoot in a wonderful display of prayer and penance. Now that is not for everyone. All are not able to do such things. But I would suggest that a more physical expression of the faith would be helpful to many, especially young people who are strong and energetic. A good pilgrimage could be a physical and communal challenge for them. Why not put some muscle and sweat into expressing our faith?"

The Spiritual Journey

"Ultimately, pilgrimage is a way to touch the inner journey and inner life. It expresses, in a sacramental way, our journey through God's world as a guest. Needless to say, your faith doesn't depend on going on an actual pilgrimage, especially to a foreign country. Time, financial resources, physical strength and health—all these may not be available for such an undertaking. Nevertheless, the principle of pilgrimage, walking and sharing and praying together, can be done, with a little imagination, on a small, local basis. And even if that is not possible, the spiritual journey must be undertaken. A virtual pilgrimage can also be taken through reading, education and creative endeavors. Learning about others' cultures with the help of books, music, art and film can lessen cultural confinement and encourage appreciation for diversity. It is possible to be a citizen of a larger world even if you are confined to your home. Our cares and concerns for others, once awakened and illumined, then will express themselves in involvement on the international, national and local scene. Christians have never been content to live only in their own backyards. The missionary impulse belongs to the Christian faith and needs to be embraced by all."

People of Place

"As I have said before, I was an alien in Ireland. I had not chosen my sojourn there as a captive. Nor was it my choosing to return as pilgrim and apostle. But I came to love those people and to identify with them. Openness to the roads that lie ahead of us in life may bring risk and even initial failure. To be a pilgrim is to trust the presence of God and to know that we are never alone in our journey. It is an attitude that touches everything in our lives. I am grateful that God's Spirit taught me the lesson well. It brought me to a new home, a new family, a new sense of place in my life.

"Know that leaving my British home and becoming a pilgrim, an alien, a displaced person never was easy for me nor would it be for the many Irish pilgrims who became missionaries after my time. The Celts were a people of place and loved the land of their birth and sustenance. The choice to leave their land and country was a deliberate choice undertaken as a way to follow Christ in love and total obedience. In the early centuries, the shedding of the martyrs' blood was, in fact, the lifeblood of the Christian Church. In my lifetime, after the time of the persecutions had ceased, the monastic life was adopted as a new way to give all for Christ. This type of life, a very ascetic and penitential one, became known among Celtic Christians as a green martyrdom. Then, another form of following Christ emerged as a response to the question.... If Christ has 'emptied himself'[4] and given up all for us, how can we be like him? This question came from a meditation on Saint Paul's words to the Philippians:

> [T]hough he was in the form of God,
> he did not regard equality with God
> as something to be exploited,
> but *emptied himself*,
> taking the form of a slave
> ...
> and became obedient to the point of death—
> even death on a cross.[5]

"The decision to voluntarily leave one's own land and country and set out for the unknown, trusting in God's providence, became known as white martyrdom. It was a new form of self-emptying, a way of giving all one's love for Christ and in imitation of him.

"The ancient pilgrims didn't leave family and land and country because they considered all that bad or evil. Nothing like that. They left them behind because they were good things they could offer to Christ in an act of love. And then most of them tended to settle down somewhere else, in a place where they hoped to die, a place they named 'the place of my resurrection.' There were few who simply kept wandering. They left the old behind but chose a new place to live. The old country was lovingly remembered and sorely missed. Perhaps the nostalgia and melancholy prevalent in the Celtic temperament has its echo, if not its cause, right here in this looking back.

"My dear friend, I am trying to get at another important point here for your consideration. Pilgrimage wasn't undertaken to find a more romantic or adventurous place. Often it wasn't even for explicitly missionary purposes. It was always to find, or return to, your own place. A sense of place is the other side to the spiritual experience of pilgrimage. They are not really opposed. They are both important. It may well be, however, that in your age which is a time of mobility, constant change and rootlessness, a sense of place also needs to be rediscovered as a spiritual source of blessing."

Journey to the Center

"To go on pilgrimage, or know oneself as pilgrim, is not to be a seeker of the extraordinary and the sensational. It is the restless, uncentered spirit that is always seeking something new, something startling and dramatic. Some who seek God and a spiritual life will immediately get up and go to a place when they hear some apparition or miracle is taking place there. But the centered, peace-filled spirit recognizes the apparitions and miracles of God in the ordinary occurrences of daily living.

"Another way to describe what I am saying is to call it a sacramental view of reality, a sacramental consciousness in daily life. God can be found right here and now. Your family, your community, your parish, your town and country—these are all the holy places where God is appearing. To live in the present, to live in the ordinary with serenity and peace may be one of the greatest miracles of our faith. To treat all the instruments and tools of our daily work with reverence because they are holy gifts of God and help us to live good and holy lives—this may require a conversion and a giving up of old, short-sighted ways. So it is that, on every new day, I called upon God's strength to direct me, God's wisdom to guide me, God's vision to light me, God's pathway before me so that I might be aware of acting, judging, deciding, seeing and walking with God.

"All of this is a way to rediscover the sense of the sacred that people once had but which is much rarer today. You live in a very secular age. Religion is regarded as a private affair, a matter of opinion. The forces of materialism and rugged individualism are the real religion in much of the culture. To have a sense of the sacred in the midst of the secular is to see things differently. Our life with God is cosmic. It includes all of life (not only the hours spent in church!). This God, a triune God, is present *in* and *through* and *in the midst of* all. Jesus once told the woman at a well in Samaria, that he wished her to know the 'gift of God' in her life.[6] That phrase rang in my ears many times in my own life as I constantly witnessed the gift of God in the ordinary workings of every day. I hope you recognize the gift of God as well. May you know this gift as you journey on pilgrimage. May you know this gift in the place of your sojourning, and finally in the place of your resurrection."

For Reflection

- How do you see your own spiritual life as a journey or a pilgrimage? Name some important milestones on that journey.

- What does being an "alien" or a "displaced person" mean to you? What do you do to welcome "aliens" in your community? When have you felt like an alien or displaced person?

- How do you allow your body to pray? In what ways does your body express your spirit at prayer?

- What things in your regular routine (e.g., books, movies, journals, music, volunteer work) express your desire to broaden your world view and help you to acquire a global consciousness?

- Think about the many things you use and touch on an ordinary day of your life. How are these sacred for you?

Closing Prayer

This day I call to me:
God's strength to direct me,
God's power to sustain me,
God's wisdom to guide me,
God's vision to light me,
God's ear to my hearing,
God's word to my speaking,
God's hand to uphold me,
God's pathway before me,
God's shield to protect me,
God's legions to save me.

Almighty and all-loving God, you know my rising and my setting. You search out my path and are acquainted with all my ways. Where can I go from your Spirit or where can I flee from your presence? You are everywhere and you are always with me. I call on you to give light to my journey and always guide and protect me whether I am at home or away.

Notes

1 *Confession*, Part III, v. 30.

2 Saint Kevin (d. 618) was the founder of the great monastic city of Glendalough in the Wicklow Mountains.

3 This story is not in the *Confession* but is found in later stories of Patrick. Tradition identifies the mountain as Croagh Patrick, Ireland's holy mountain near Westport on Clew Bay in County Mayo.

4 This was known as the *kenosis*, or self-emptying, of Christ.

5 Philippians 2:6-11. This was probably an even more ancient hymn quoted by Paul.

6 John 4:10.

DAY SIX
In the Valley of the Shadow of Death

Coming Together in the Spirit

I recently read the story of a man who decided to spend the winter on an ice boat in the Arctic Circle below the North Pole.[1] It is a story of a man coping with long months of cold and darkness, as well as with loneliness and fear. He wanted to experience life as the Inuits do. He learned that standing before the great Ice Bear was part of an adult rite of passage. The narration reaches its climax in an encounter of the protagonist with a polar bear. Coming behind the bear, he called out his name, "Nanook." As the bear whirled around and faced him, the man dropped his rifle and they stared at each other. His time in the darkness, he writes, was a preparation for this moment. And then, the story continues,

> I took one more step. The bear grunted and rocked forward. I opened my arms, turning my palms to the heavens. The bear stepped toward me. He rose above me, a horrible mountain of fang and claw, crushing power and lightning speed. The moment hung in its own eternity. And then the bear spun around and slid away in great strides over the tundra. I stood stunned and faint, my soul indelibly

embossed with the bear's message: "Here, I give
you back your life. It has been washed pure by your
own fear. Enjoy it deeply, learn from it daily, and use
it wisely, for there is a purpose larger than
yourself."[2]

I believe this story is a model of the spiritual life. The
author relives what many ancient monks did in going to
the desolation of the desert. The purpose of such a
journey, undertaken by many an Irish monk, was to face
the darkness and fears within, identified as demons, and
to stare them down.

The complexity and instability of modern life have
resulted in the tendency to seek simplistic and
fundamentalist answers and solutions. So there is a whole
melange of remedies available now, some of which can
only be labeled "Spirituality lite." Some of the New Age
spiritualities, as well as even some Christian spiritualities,
fall into this category. In some of these systems, all is
light; there is no darkness. All is comforting; there is no
challenge. One doesn't face the bear but turns in flight
and busyness. Religion becomes a practice to make one
feel good.

The deeper Christian tradition has always been more
paradoxical and challenging. The shadow of the cross is
ever present. The paschal mystery, the death and rising of
Christ from the dead, is the principal paradigm for
understanding our own journey and pilgrimage. There
can be no growth in the Spirit without accompanying
Christ through the "valley of the shadow of darkness."
Any spirituality that promises only light is not dealing
with reality. Christianity is a religion of martyrs, of heroes
and heroines, of courageous and committed people who
have lived with conflict and contradiction in their
following of Christ.

Defining Our Thematic Context

Our retreat with Patrick today turns to the dark side of our spiritual lives. Patrick's own story was full of darkness—slavery, imprisonment, betrayal, threatening natural forces, hunger, cold and near nakedness. He has always been loved by the Irish because he has experienced, like them, the pain of exile, insecurity, poverty and oppression. For centuries the Irish (as well as the Welsh and Scots) have been a marginalized people, persecuted and pushed to the point of extinction. They rallied to Patrick in gratitude for the gift of faith in the Christ who has suffered with them as he did with Patrick. Today, we reflect with our director on the various strains of darkness in our life and how, in faith, hope and courage, we can deal with them.

Opening Prayer

This day I call on all these heavenly powers to protect
    me:
from snares of the demon
from evil enticements
from failings of nature
from one person or many
who try to destroy me anear or afar.

Around me I gather these forces to save my soul and
    my body
from dark powers that assail me:
against false prophesyings,
against pagan devisings,
against heretical lying,
and false gods all around me.

Almighty and all-protecting God, life is often dark

and I am unsure of the path before me. Much of what happens around me just seems too much to endure and at times I feel lost on my journey. Help me to trust the Good Shepherd who guides me along the right paths. May I always know your protecting presence in the courage and faith that your Spirit brings. May I walk through the valley of the shadow of darkness and not be afraid knowing you are near.

RETREAT SESSION SIX
Cosmic, Personal and Spiritual Darkness

"Today, my dear friend, I want to reflect with you on the dark side of reality and how that influences our spiritual journey. I lived in a climate that was marked by long, dark and cold winters. People coped the best they could and adapted as was necessary. But I also experienced much interior darkness and coldness. The Lord allowed me to intimately share with him in joys, his sonship, his preaching and teaching. And I also felt close to Christ in his sufferings. I am certain I was not unique. Often we try to avoid the dark areas in our lives. We 'turn on the lights' when it gets too dark. Sometimes that is a wise thing to do. Sometimes it is an avoidance of seeing the other side of reality."

Dark Side of Nature

"Earlier in the week we meditated on the holiness of creation and the challenge of finding God in the goodness of creation. But even then we alluded to the fact that there is a dark side to nature. There is a tremendous energy and power in creation that, at times, seems to turn against human beings. Tornadoes, hurricanes, earthquakes, ice storms, droughts, famines and floods threaten us. The ancient Celts, like many primitive peoples, tried to work with nature and cooperate with it, wanting to understand its ways as best they could. But they also tried to placate nature in the belief that it was inhabited by petty and jealous gods whom they needed as allies.

"Christian Celts, true to the heritage of their ancestors, continued to live and work in harmony with nature, recognizing the power of God manifested in it. As an agrarian people, they knew that seeds had to die to bring forth new fruit, that one level of the animal world fed on another. They respected the power of creation as a mystery of life that was only partially understood. They knew that they had much to learn from nature. They also prayed fervently to be protected from the dark powers of creation. Protection prayers are part of the rich Celtic heritage. 'Lorica,' or breastplates, are prayers calling on the protective power of God. The 'cairn' was a practice whereby people drew a circle around themselves and called on the Trinity for protection. Many mantric-like litanies repeated phrases that echoed a heartbeat or the repetitive striking of the breast in sorrow as the pray-er sought harmony with spiritual powers to deal with material forces.

"I had grown up with this kind of awareness and communication with nature. But my experience of six years as a slave in Ireland brought a deeper appreciation of what this really meant. The nights were long and often cold. Rain was a frequent occurrence and snow and ice were not uncommon. I had only a few animal skins to protect my body. An occasional storm blew off the

western sea with a ferocity that made me doubt that I
could survive. A sunny, warm day became a real gift to
treasure. I would then go down to the water to bathe. The
sea, usually a friend, could also show its dark side. Once,
when enjoying the cleansing waters, I was caught by an
undertow and was almost washed out to sea. I had
relaxed my guard against the powers of the mighty
waters. I learned to pray to be protected from those dark
powers of nature ever afterwards.

"[T]he most holy God has often freed me from slavery and
from twelve perils whereby my soul was endangered, besides
numerous treacheries and things which I am unable to express
in words.... And if I should be worthy, I am prepared to give up
even my life unhesitatingly and most gladly for his name.[3]

"You live in the same world I did, surrounded by and
immersed in the beauty and power of God's creation. You
have, however, both an advantage and a disadvantage
which I did not have. The people of your time, a scientific
age unlike my own, have a greater understanding of the
movements and forces of nature. When disaster threatens,
you can prepare yourselves more effectively. But you are
also cut off from intimacy with these powers. Your well-
built homes and other comforts, such as electric lights and
central heating, insulate you from the primal powers of
creation. You are apt to miss the rhythms of creation and
live as though you, yourself, were not part of that
creation.

"Worse than that, when some natural disaster strikes,
you are even more at the mercy of these forces than we
were. I sadly observe how many in the present era
become insulted, even outraged, by a God who would
release such powers on the world and on human beings.
Failing to honor the mystery of God's creation, people are
more prone to be shaken by the dark side of the same
natural world. Though you will never fully solve the

mystery of creation, you can certainly help yourself by
rediscovering a harmony with God and all that God has
made. Respect and reverence for the cosmos is the first
lesson in learning to live with it. On the other hand, an
attitude of domination of the world and unlimited use of
creation's resources leads us to think we can control it,
and that only leads to disaster."

Human Pain and Suffering

"Perhaps, much more difficult, is understanding and
accepting the mystery of human suffering, especially
when it impacts the lives of infants, children and young
people. Sorrow, grief, pain and disease, as well as death,
are all part of human existence. They can be destructive of
the human spirit. But they can also help us to grow in
compassion. Accepting the inevitability of human
suffering does not mean that we should not try to
alleviate it and, when possible, prevent it. Primitive
peoples used herbs and other natural remedies to deal
with illness. Thanks to science and medical technology
you have many more means at your disposal to prolong
life and cure illness. That is a sign that you are using well
the gifts God has given you in creation.

"But you still can't control the natural world, and the
human body is part of that mystery. Thinking that science
has all the answers can lead to anger, frustration and
disillusionment when faced with premature death or
incurable illness. Science does not have all the answers.
The human being is a whole and that means there are
emotional and spiritual sides to us as well. Prayer,
humility, an awareness of mortality and human
vulnerability before God may also be needed remedies. It
is only by clinging to faith and hope in a God who is
close and loving that we can overcome tragedy,

transforming it into a means of growth. I am not advising just a resignation to fate, but an acceptance and openness to all of life, even to its pain. Transformation occurs when, in solidarity with the Christ who suffers with us, we become less controlling, less self-centered, more loving and more compassionate.

"In the end, it all comes down to the fact that God is the center of this creation and we are not. God is in control and we are not. That seems to be a very difficult lesson for humans of any time to learn. We would rather have all as light and eradicate the darkness. But, as Christians, we believe that even our darkness and our pain are redemptive. I am consoled by the words of Saint Paul: 'I am now rejoicing in my sufferings for your sake, and in my flesh I am completing what is lacking in Christ's afflictions for the sake of his body, that is, the church.'[4] Everyone, even the sick and invalid, thus contributes to the redemption of the world while working out his or her own salvation."

Darkness of Human Relationships

"I think the much more difficult and painful parts of the dark side of life occur in our relationships with one another. Human beings are capable of great love and great courage. They are also capable of shocking hatred and savagery. Wars, violence, greed, selfishness, oppression of one people over another, genocide, slavery, poverty—these are all part of human history. The wild beasts that my people feared have been replaced by crime, drugs, radioactive waste, the pollution of the air and water. Many persons are selfish and destroy the very gifts of God. On a more intimate and individual level, humans suffer from betrayals, rejections, desolation and depression, loneliness and isolation.

"Poverty and loneliness were part of my experience

of slavery and exile. The lack of normal family and human relationships forever scarred me. I experienced periods of sadness and depression, feeling there was no hope that things would improve. Later, all of this paled in comparison to the rejection and betrayal I endured at the hands of my peers and superiors.

"I was tried by a number of my elders who came and cast up my sins as a charge against my laborious episcopate.... I was vigorously overwhelmed to the point of falling here and for eternity, but the Lord spared the sojourner in exile because of his own kindly name, and he came powerfully to my support in this crushing under heel.[5]

"I had given up everything, after returning to my home, to follow Christ. With the encouragement of others, I had been ordained a priest. Then I was chosen to be a bishop and confirmed in my call to return to the Irish to bring the gospel to them. I labored hard, had no permanent domicile, was never able to settle down in any comfort, suffered imprisonment and other indignities. But all of this, with Saint Paul, I did gladly for the sake of Christ.

"Then my ecclesiastical peers back in Britain began to criticize everything I did. I was accused of being too rustic and unlearned for my task and of bringing ignominy on the Church and the episcopate. I was accused of taking gifts and living on others' money. Then came the crowning blow. A former friend, a priest who had in fact argued the case for my being sent to the Irish, betrayed me. He broadcast a secret sin that I had confessed to him in my youth, prior to my being taken in slavery. I had been enticed and challenged to take part in a Roman pagan sacrifice and my curiosity led me to betray my faith.[6] This youthful sin was made public and used to discredit me. I considered giving up my mission and returning to Britain. However, a soul friend helped me to see that jealousy and revenge were the driving forces behind these accusations. My letter to Coroticus, condemning him for the kidnapping of Irish youths into slavery, was an embarrassment to many in Britain.[7] The authorities in Britain would not criticize Coroticus for they themselves had slaves. And they were jealous of the success of my mission to the Irish.

"That was a dark time for me. Have you ever experienced anything like that? Have your efforts, made in good will and zeal, been criticized and perhaps even condemned by others in your own profession, by others in the Church or in your own community or family? Why must life become so difficult when you are trying to accomplish something? Why does God allow such a thing to happen? All of this is part of the dark side of life that can't be fully explained. But the example of Christ in his facing evil with love gives the Christian disciple a marvelous paradigm to imitate. In love, we, too, can embrace the pain of living in truth and integrity. We accept the full mystery of human existence which has been made divine by Christ living it with us."

Darkness of the Human Heart

"Christians of my time also prayed for protection against dangers to the soul: false prophesyings, pagan devisings, heretical lying. You have these in a more insidious form today: false advertising, consumerism, racism, sexism, militarism and other social sins that poison the culture. You breathe in dark influences and often don't even know it. And this leads us to consider another level of the darkness in life. This is the level many would prefer to ignore—and often they are successful in doing so. This is the darkness that lies within the human heart, that is found in each one of us.

We all try to cover it up. We deny it. We project it on others. We blame others. But it remains there like a festering wound that is ignored. Human beings are rather insecure creatures and don't deal well with weakness, vulnerability and imperfection in themselves. We so often ignore the fears, the prejudices, the addictions and compulsions, the nagging feelings of anger, sadness, jealousy and lust that lurk in the heart. It is not that I want to imply that we are evil, nor do I want to create an atmosphere of guilt and shame. It is simply to acknowledge that we live in a sin-scarred world and that sin pervades all who are part of the world.

"For many this sin lies on a subconscious or unconscious level and awaits to be recognized and dealt with. It needs to be named, to be claimed, to be tamed so that its energy might be redirected. Penances and the ascetical life have had the purpose of aiding this taming and purifying process. Yes, the darkness lurks. The tendency is to find a way of ignoring it, a way of smothering it. But the darkness must be brought into the light. Sin and the frailty of the human condition must be acknowledged. This is the path to freedom and healing. And I think it is also the opening to deal with all the other darknesses that we have discussed above.

"*I do not trust myself, as long as I am in this body of death, because he is strong who strives daily to turn me way from the faith and from that chastity of an unfeigned religion which I have proposed to keep, to the end of my life for the Lord.*"[8]

Soul Friends and Penance

"The Celtic tradition of the soul friend led to the practice of private penance in the Sacrament of Reconciliation. Unfortunately, this sacrament later became a mechanical and external practice for many people. The need for a real soul friend, however, remains vital to facing realistically the darkness in our lives. We attempt to bring light to our darkness and can do this in prayer and meditation, when we allow all the dark corners of the soul to come into the light of our awareness. But then we need to articulate this awareness. Sharing with a soul friend is helpful. Confession to God, put in words to another, is healing. The occasional celebration of God's mercy and forgiveness in the Sacrament of Reconciliation assures us of God's merciful and loving presence even in the darkness of our hearts."

Darkness of Death

"We must face one final area of darkness in human life—death. A Christian lives in faith and hope before passing beyond his or her death. From what we actually know from life's experience, all seems to be dark on the other side of that passing. But the Risen Lord, the first fruits of the new creation, is the assurance of our own resurrection. I have more than once, in these days, alluded to the 'place of one's resurrection.' So did faithful Celtic Christians speak and think of their death. The emphasis was not on the death but on the resurrection. They received from their pagan ancestors a keen sense of the closeness of the other world and were not afraid of it. As Christians, we are even more aware that one may face one's fears about darkness and the unknown because Christ did the same before us. As the blessed apostle put it:

> For [Christ] must reign until he has put all his enemies under his feet. The last enemy to be destroyed is death. For God has put all things in subjection under his feet.[9]

"Christians are grateful, too, for the many saints who

have shown their courage before death and their eagerness to share in the Resurrection of the Christ. They showed us that death, including the daily death involved in our ongoing transformation, is the path to resurrection."

The Celtic High Cross

"The high cross, found in Ireland and other Celtic Christian countries, is a monument that proclaims the Celtic intertwining of life, death and resurrection. These spectacularly large crosses were decorated with events from the life of Christ and other biblical figures and saints. Truly, the shadow of the cross lay across the country and reminded Christians over the centuries that Christ suffered with them.

"But these high crosses are also noted for the circle around the crossbeams. The circle is a symbol of the sun. It is also the victory wreath of Christ the Risen One. As I once cried tears of compunction when I finally discovered how good and merciful God was to me, these crosses have likewise prompted in many others a loving identification with and gratitude to a God who entered the darkness with his people and emerged victorious.

"My dear friend, I hope this day's reflection has not been too desolate for you to consider. I have waited until this day to address the dark side of reality. I am confident that, having reflected in the previous days on the intimate presence of God, the saints and angels, and on our own incorporation into the life of Christ, you can overcome your fears and hesitancies in looking at this darkness. No, I don't have all the answers for you. You must simply live in faith with the mystery of life. The paschal mystery is the only key I can give you. Christ, your Lord and brother, died for you and with you. Thus you can die for him and with him. Daily you can die to sin and selfishness and rise to new life. If you can face death, can you not face life in its many challenges and uncertainties as well? You are called to live fully and accept your own humanity which is prone to weakness and to sin. Jesus assures us, 'Do not be afraid, for I am with you.'"

For Reflection

- *Have you ever been told, in the face of adversity, to simply "Offer it up"? What in Patrick's words could help you to get beyond a stoic acceptance of suffering?*

- *How do you deal with the death of a young child from a disease like leukemia?*

- *What place does the cross have in your spirituality? And the risen Christ?*

- *How do you name sin and what are its effects in your life?*

- *What fears, prejudices, compulsions and addictions are in your life? How do you bring them into the light?*

Closing Prayer

This day I call on all these powers to protect me:
from snares of the demon
from evil enticements
from failings of nature
from one person or many
who try to destroy me anear or afar.

Around me I gather these forces to save my soul and
   my body
from dark powers that assail me:
against false prophesyings,

against pagan devisings,
against heretical lying,
and false gods all around me.

Almighty God, I thank you for the light to face the
darkness in my life. Help me to overcome the fears I have
of looking at the dark in the world and in my soul. May
your Spirit give me faith and courage to walk with Christ
my Savior on the path to new life.

Notes

[1] The story is recounted by Alvah Simon in his *North to the Night:
A Year in the Arctic Ice* (Camden, Me.: International Marine, 1998).

[2] Simon, p. 311.

[3] *Confession*, Part III, v. 35, 37.

[4] Colossians 1:24.

[5] *Confession*, Part III, v. 26.

[6] This is a conjecture, as Patrick does not tell us what that sin had
been. At the time there were only three major sins—apostasy,
murder and adultery. At his age and in his setting, the first is the
most likely for Patrick to have committed. See Máire B. dePaor,
p. 150.

[7] See "Letter to Coroticus," particularly paragraph III.

[8] *Confession*, Part IV, v. 43.

[9] 1 Corinthians 15:25-27.

DAY SEVEN
Knowing the Cosmic Christ

Coming Together in the Spirit

Pierre Teilhard de Chardin (1881-1955) was a French Jesuit. He was born and grew up in the Auvergne area of France, an area of massive rocks, mountains and extinct volcanoes. This locale was once the heart of Celtic Gaul. Chardin's theological studies led him to Saint Paul and a vision of Christ that he called "cosmic." His scientific studies in geology, anthropology and paleontology opened up a view of humanity and the universe that impressed him with its vastness and depth. His ensuing vision of the future of humanity brought the Cosmic Christ and an evolutionary universe into harmony.

> Glorious Lord Jesus: ...power as implacable as the world and as warm as life; you whose forehead is of the whiteness of snow, whose eyes are of fire, and whose feet are brighter than molten gold; you whose hands imprison the stars; you who are the first and last, the living and the dead and the risen again; you who gather into your exuberant unity every beauty, every affinity, every energy, every mode of existence; it is you to whom my being cried out with a desire as vast as the universe, "In truth you are my Lord and my God."[1]

Like Patrick, Chardin found himself a pilgrim on the earth, traveling to Asia, Africa and North America in the pursuit of his mission. He died, in exile, in New York on Easter Sunday fulfilling his wish to die on the day of the Resurrection. Like Patrick he was criticized by his native ecclesiastical peers and superiors. Nothing of his writings, extensive as they were, was printed until after his death.

Chardin's view of the Christ finds an echo in the early Church in which the Pauline doctrine of the Mystical Body was so central. I believe we have seen this perspective in Patrick, though the apostle to Ireland certainly did not proclaim the "Cosmic Christ" as such. But, on this last day of our retreat with Saint Patrick, we must consider how this theme has been central to our reflections.

Patrick has given you some new perspectives on your spiritual life. Have you noticed that we have heard little of the piety and devotionalism that many associate with Irish spirituality? What we have been hearing is a challenging call to mature faith. This is not just about going to Mass on Sunday and keeping some rules. This is an all-encompassing spirituality that touches every movement of every day. It has been said that the Celts were a God-intoxicated people. Others have described their spirituality as passionate and even fierce, especially as evidenced in some of its asceticism. It has been a warrior's faith, a hero's journey. But there is also the gentle side expressed in a poetry that is sweet and in the emphasis on intimacy and relationship. Today, Patrick returns us to the center of this spirituality—the person of the Christ.

Defining Our Thematic Context

The final stanza of the "Breastplate of Saint Patrick" extols the protective power of the Christ. This is the only stanza of this beautiful prayer which is known to many people and has even been put to music in various forms. We can better appreciate now, after praying the previous six stanzas, that it is really the climax of this longer poem prayer with its extensive vision of God's creative presence in the universe. This final stanza brings together much of what Patrick has been speaking about all week and focuses on our theme of the Cosmic Christ.

Opening Prayer

Be Christ this day my strong protector;
Christ beside me, Christ before me;
Christ behind me, Christ within me;
Christ beneath me, Christ above me;
Christ to right of me, Christ to left of me;
Christ in my lying, my sitting, my rising;
Christ in heart of all who know me,
Christ on tongue of all who meet me,
Christ in eye of all who see me,
Christ in ear of all who hear me.

Praise to you, all holy Three-in-One God. Praise to you, Father, from whom all life and blessings come. Praise to you, Lord Jesus Christ, eternal Word and the first fruits of the new creation. Praise to you, Holy Spirit, who breathes within me as you breathed within the Christ, allowing me to call out, "Abba, Father."

Retreat Session Seven
I Live, Not I, But Christ Lives in Me

"Dear friend, it has been a pleasant seven days sharing these memories and reflections with you. Today I'd like to revisit some of what we have shared and leave you with some perspectives for your own spiritual journey. I, Patrick, have looked back to my own experience of growing as a Christian; I have also had the luxury of looking at it through the lens of fifteen hundred years of Church history. On this seventh day, I want to focus on our theme of knowing the Cosmic Christ. It has been an underlying motif in all these days and I want to emphasize that now.

"Without any doubt we will rise again on that day in the brightness of the sun, that is to say, in the glory of Christ Jesus our Redeemer, as 'children of the living God' and 'joint heirs with Christ,' and 'about to be conformed to his image,' since 'from him and through him and in him we are to reign...'. We believe and adore the true sun, Christ, who will never die; nor will he 'who does his will' but will live forever, as Christ also lives forever, he who reigns with God the Almighty Father, and with the Holy Spirit before the ages, and now and forever. Amen."[2]

The Cosmic Christ Throughout This Retreat

"Our retreat started with a day of prayer that confessed our faith in a triune God, creator of a good world, intimately close to us in all we do. As Christians, our belief in the Holy Trinity is a central and essential tenet of faith. But it is not just a doctrine. It is the very secret to life and the universe. Our God is not isolated and alone. Our God is a community, is relationship, is interactive by nature and being. And we are called to share in that life. Baptized in the name of that Trinity, each one of us began a journey ever deeper into the mystery of that triune God.

"But no one of us could approach that triune God unless we were given an opening for our human, created, limited and mortal selves to enter. That doorway, that very way, that truth, that life for us is the Christ. On our second day, therefore, we considered ways to get to know Christ, to get to know the mind of Christ, to enter into relationship with him.

"This Christ is not just a memory of someone who lived two millennia ago. The Christ we believe and profess is a living Christ, the risen Lord, the first fruits of a new creation to which we are invited. Our task is to help build and enjoy this new creation which is the Kingdom of God. Christ has broken the limitations of humanity and of all of the material universe. This is the Cosmic Christ, the One who has assumed all of creation into himself. We now form his Body. The doctrine of the Mystical Body of Christ, based on the insights of Saint Paul, remains a powerful image for us to get to know and love the Christ. Since the Vatican Council, theologians have spoken of the Church more in terms of the 'People of God.' This is a good, living image. But the image of the Mystical Body is also still a powerful one for you to reflect on as well. It includes not only us but the angels and saints and all who have gone before us.

"Our intimacy with the living angels and saints was the topic of our third day together. But how could they be living with us and be accompanying us together in our journey, if they were not, as well, members of the Body of Christ? So the Cosmic Christ is also our contact with the spiritual world. In the perfect union of his physical body and human soul in the Godhead, he is our passageway to the spiritual world, the other world. Already, here on earth, we share the life of God with the angels, saints and all our ancestors.

"One important conclusion to this worldview is our need to trust in the presence of the spiritual world, to be open to the presence of the angels and saints in our hearts and souls. I have spoken, at times of the 'spiritual senses' that are within us, analogous to the external senses. Nourishing our spiritual life through prayer, reading, meditation and works of compassion opens up those senses to be able to apprehend the spiritual.

"On the fourth day we looked at the material universe, the created cosmos which was created through the Word at the beginning of time and has always been good. Now, after the Resurrection and the new creation, this universe is eternally wedded to God through the Christ. In the Ascension, a corporeal, human person has forever entered into the heart of God. We also believe that Mary, mother of the Christ and, therefore, our mother, too, has been taken bodily to the triune God. There is a sacredness to creation and material being that demands our reverence, our respect and our care. It is our spiritual senses, again, that allow the external senses to recognize the sacredness of matter and to treat the created things of our everyday existence with prayerful reverence.

"When we came together for our fifth day of retreat, our approach shifted a bit. We changed the emphasis from the persons with whom we share our spiritual journey to some aspects of the journey itself. How do we walk in Christ? How do we live in Christ? Our reflections centered on two perspectives. First, we looked at pilgrimage as a very human and incarnational way to live the spiritual journey. Then we balanced this by looking at the importance of being rooted in place, in apprehending the sacredness of the here and now. The reality of the Risen Lord, the new creation, the Cosmic Christ, opens us to a sacramental consciousness. The ordinary becomes extraordinary and is revelatory of the mystery of the triune God.

"Yesterday, the sixth day, was a time for us to look at the dark side of the journey. We were describing what is really a universal battle in which we are asked to take our place. The Cosmic Christ has conquered sin and death but the fruits of this victory must be accepted and assimilated by his Body. Not until the day when all has been brought under his sway and all creation has been "recapitulated in Christ"[3] and he has returned all of this creation back to the Father from whence it came, will the battle be complete. Then, through Christ, the image of paradise which Adam and Eve enjoyed in the garden, will be a reality.

"Meanwhile, we live with the ongoing battle against the powers of evil. Nature still groans to be fully free and redeemed and bares its dark side in destructive ways. Individual human beings, as well as nations, destroy and violently oppress each other. And, since we are all part of one Body, when one part of the body suffers, it will be felt elsewhere and everywhere. If the children of Bosnia or Palestine or Northern Ireland suffer violence, then the children of America and Australia and England will also be affected. It may seem unjust that the innocent suffer but that happens because we are all part of one human family, one Body of Christ. No one is an island.

"Where does that leave us at the end of this week? I lived at a time when many people thought the end of the world was near. The breakdown of the Roman Empire plunged much of Europe into a dark age and many thought it would be the end of time. This feeling recurs often and has dominated culture about every four hundred years. It is with you again today at the dawn of the third millennium. But no one knows the day nor the hour when any sort of ending may occur. Our belief in the Cosmic Christ, however, directs our thoughts and actions elsewhere. I would like to focus in today's final retreat reflection on the Eucharist and how we see the world as 'cosmic' Christians."

The Eucharist and the Cosmic Christ

"The Holy Eucharist is the heart of our communal life as Christians and as Church. It is the sacramental renewal of our being brought into the life of the Holy Trinity at our Baptism. It is our participation in the life of Christ as his Body on earth. The renewal of the liturgy that has come to the Church since the Second Vatican Council has brought back this understanding of the cosmic and mystical meaning of the Eucharist. No doubt your parents never would have thought of it in this way. The Eucharist had become, prior to the Council, a very individualized and passive affair. The accent was on the individual Christian attending the Mass where the priest reenacted the sacrifice of Calvary. Then each layperson was able to receive the fruit of that sacrifice in Holy Communion.

"The experience of the Mass in the centuries after the Protestant Reformation and the Council of Trent had gradually become this kind of privatized and passive worship. The Irish Catholic experience contributed to it greatly inasmuch as the people's participation in the Mass had to become very quiet and hidden. First, in the times of the Cromwellian persecutions, and then, when the Mass was outlawed in the penal times, Irish Catholics gathered secretly, often in darkness. They were simply present while the priest (perhaps even unseen in another room) performed the Mass for them. Meanwhile, the lay attendees quietly recited the Rosary or other prayers.

Great faith and courage were expressed in this fidelity to the Eucharist. But it also led to the loss of any sense of active and communal participation. The Council brought that back to the Church.

"In the Eucharist the covenant of Baptism is renewed. In the Eucharist each person present offers his or her own life and work as a sacrifice to the Father in union with Christ through the power of the Holy Spirit. When the ordained priest, uniting the participants in union with the Church throughout the world, calls on the power of the Spirit to change the elements into the Body of Christ, he is praying that invocation over all the people as well as over the bread. The fact that the bread becomes the Body of Christ is the great sign and assurance that the people, too, will become the Body of Christ. All that we do throughout the week becomes priestly inasmuch as all we do is an act of worship, whether as parent, worker or invalid. Then, at Mass, we bring our lives together and offer them in union with Christ our head, and with the whole Church. There we join the angels and the saints and all our ancestors in worship. There all of creation is lifted up through the signs of bread and wine, the human word and human touch. There we may dare to face the dark forces of the cosmos and pray for protection in our cosmic battle against evil.

"So the Eucharist is the great and visible sign to us of the reality of the new creation, the presence of the risen Lord as the Cosmic Christ that is discernible through the eyes of faith. With such a gift and such a power we can then go forth to our everyday life where we live out our Christian discipleship which means building the Kingdom of God and engaging in a battle against the powers of evil."

The Choice and Challenge of Our Faith
in the Cosmic Christ

"Before I leave you, my good friend, I want to express my belief that each of us has a choice in the basic stance we take toward life and this world. It concerns the vision you have of reality and what you believe is possible. My world of the fifth century was fraught with difficulties, and we Christians tried to respond to them as we understood them. Since survival was such a basic need, and our resources much fewer, it was simpler for us to be focused on the battle. The challenge for you is to recognize the cosmic nature of the battle and then to respond accordingly, which may be much more demanding for your generation. But the Christ with all his saints and angels are with you, bringing you into union with the triune God. And so I dare lay before you a choice of visions and the challenge to respond.

"As I look on the world and the Church at the beginning of the third millennium of Christianity, I perceive there are great forces of darkness and disintegration as well as hopeful forces of light and integration. What do I mean by that? Let me try to draw a picture for you.

"First, let me explain what I mean by 'the forces of disintegration.' Your world is largely a 'me culture' concerned with maximum self-fulfillment often without regard to what that means for others, whether those others are your neighbors, people in other parts of the globe or even nature itself. Related to a strong individualism is an equally strong tribalism and nationalism that pits one group of people against another. You have witnessed this in the former Yugoslavia, in the Middle East (land of Jesus' birth) and in Ireland itself. Another symptom of this culture is a rampant consumerism with the acquisition of things (cars, houses, gadgets, toys) that promise to give people meaning but only lead to a demand for more things. Things are more important than people and human life is neglected through the dark powers of abortion, child neglect, euthanasia and capital punishment. A greed which leads to violence often follows.

"Let me name a few more of these negative powers. Individual freedom and the right to choose are the only prevalent, widely held values. There is little sense of the common good and the demand, at times, to sacrifice oneself for it. There is an increase of suicide among young people in many areas. There is a sense of exhaustion, a loss of feeling, minimal expectations of others, minimal hopes. Serious things such as worship and public discourse are turned into entertainment, and there is a widespread desire to parody and mock everything. There is much isolation, loneliness and a lack of connection with others. There is a failure to keep, perhaps even an ability to keep, commitments. You may add racism, sexism, the decline of urban centers, concern about radioactive fallout, and so on and so on. I don't want to depress you, but this is what I mean by naming the darkness. You surely need a breastplate, a protection from many of these forces.

"However, I believe there are stronger forces of integration in your midst as well. I believe the world is still basically good because it is God's creation, and it is a redeemed world because of Christ's saving work. Let me name some of the positive forces that I perceive. It is becoming clearer and daily more obvious that all are mutually interrelated—God, people, the earth. Ever since the first astronauts looked back at earth from space, you have been able to actually see the oneness and interconnection of your planet, as well as its fragility. A global consciousness is emerging.

"People are teaching a global ethic. Ideologies such as communism and apartheid are collapsing. There is a growing sensibility to the sins of sexism, racism, consumerism and nationalism accompanied by a growing desire to heal them. Human rights and liberation for all have become international concerns. There is a growing concern for the earth and for the common good (not just 'my good'). There is a spiritual hunger evident in a proliferation of serious spiritual books and literature, meditation groups that meet, retreat houses that are full. There is a growing army of volunteers who perform services to help others in need.

"There is also a growing global awareness and the sharing of knowledge evident in the expansion of the Internet and the media. There is openness of religions to each other and a new tolerance for differences. None of this demands that you give up your own faith in Christ as the unique mediator I have described. In fact, other religions may help Christians understand aspects of the Christ to which they have not paid much attention.

"I am sure you can name other good forces at work in the world today to add to these. The question is which set of values, which of the above visions, best corresponds to the Kingdom of the Cosmic Christ? It is clear with which forces the Christ stands. The second group, that of light, is a Trinitarian consciousness that fosters unity and relationship, and rejects isolation and separation. This second group of forces can be seen to be at play in the parables of the Kingdom which Jesus taught.

"Which vision do you choose? Which vision do you want to pass on to your children? Each person opts for one or the other, not just by words, but by deeds and life-style. If you recognize yourself as a part and microcosm of all creation, if you know that you are related, connected and responsible for all, then you know that everything you do or fail to do affects the whole. Your decision to read, to study, to pray, to know what is going on, to take part in local community, the Church, the country, all contribute to light and integration. And your decision not to care, not to be involved, not to read and form an educated understanding—this is a vote for the powers of darkness.

"I believe people owe it to their children to be people of hope, visionaries of a better world. This new world won't come automatically. It might not even come in your own lifetime. Things might get worse before they get better. The old selfish and dark ways may have to die a slow death before new life comes. But God the Father calls all into a future with his Christ, nourished by the Spirit. We must not retreat into a nostalgic past which one bitterly bemoans as lost and thus evades doing what is required now. Our faith in God allows us to move into the future with hope.

"Whence moreover 'shall I return to him for all his bounty to me?' But what shall I say or what shall I promise to my Lord? For I can do nothing unless he himself enables me; but 'he tests the hearts and minds,' and 'I have eagerly desired,' and 'I was ready' that he should grant to me 'to drink his cup,' just as he granted to others who loved him. Wherefore 'may it never happen to me' from my God that I should ever lose his own people 'whom he has formed' for himself at the ends of the earth.

"I pray God that he may grant me perseverance and to grant that I may be a faithful witness to him up to the point of death for the sake of my God. And if I ever imitated anything good for the sake of my God whom I love dearly, I pray him to grant to me that with those sojourners and captives for his name's sake I may shed my blood....

"I beseech those who believe in and fear God, whoever is pleased to look at or receive this writing, which Patrick, a sinner, untaught, has composed in Ireland, that if I have

*accomplished or demonstrated any small thing according to
God's good pleasure; let this be your conclusion and it must be
most truly believed that it was 'the gift of God.' And this is my
confession before I die."*[4]

For Reflection

- *As you consider these two visions of light and darkness,
  which vision do you live out in your daily life? Name some
  specific ways that you choose one or the other vision.*

- *Is the Eucharist the important center of your life with
  Christ? Is there anything in Patrick's description of it that
  might enhance how you celebrate this sacrament?*

- *Looking back at the seven days of this retreat, what have
  you found to be most striking or significant? What do you
  take with you? What might challenge you to more
  reflection or action?*

Closing Prayer

Be Christ this day my strong protector;
Christ beside me, Christ before me;
Christ behind me, Christ within me;
Christ beneath me, Christ above me;
Christ to right of me, Christ to left of me;
Christ in my lying, my sitting, my rising;
Christ in heart of all who know me;
Christ on tongue of all who meet me,
Christ in eye of all who see me,
Christ in ear of all who hear me.

For my shield this day I call a mighty power:
the Holy Trinity! Affirming threeness, confessing
    oneness

in the making of all—through love—
For to the Lord belongs salvation
and to the Lord belongs salvation
and to Christ belongs salvation.

May your salvation, Lord, be with us always. Amen.

Notes

[1] Pierre Teilhard de Chardin, *The Heart of Matter* (New York: Harcourt Brace Jovanovich, 1980), p. 131.

[2] *Confession*, Part V, v. 59-60.

[3] This phrase goes back to Saint Irenaeus of Lyons (130-200) and expresses a theology of the early Church that expressed the summit of human evolution is summed up in the humanity of the Christ. It is very conceivable that Patrick also shared this viewpoint. The same idea was also taken up by Chardin.

[4] *Confession*, Part V, v. 57-58, 62.

Going Forth to Live the Theme

"My dear friend, it is time to bring our retreat to an end. I have shared my story and the lessons learned from my life in Christ to suggest some ways to look at your own spiritual life and the world you live in today. I had to bring the Christian message to a society and culture that did not know Christ. You no longer have the support of national, ethnic or even family connections to help you be a good Christian or lead others to Christianity. It is only through a personal and committed faith in the Christ that you will preserve your faith. But you are not alone in this faith. I hope our retreat has reinforced your faith in the presence of many spiritual presences that guide you and support you in your own spiritual journey.

"It has been a delight to spend this time with you. Remember, that I will be walking with you along with Christ, Mary, all the saints and your beloved ancestors. Together, encompassed in a loving triune God, we are here for you. If you want to talk to me any time in prayer, I will welcome your continued friendship."

Deepening Your Acquaintance

The following books and resources are intended to help retreatants sustain their relationship with Patrick. Additional resources are offered for those who want to explore both Celtic spirituality and the theme of the Cosmic Christ in other contexts.

Books

Adam, David, *The Cry of the Deer: Meditations on the Hymn of St. Patrick* (Wilton, Conn.: Morehouse-Barlow, 1987). Meditations on the Breastplate.

De Paor, Liam, *Saint Patrick's World: The Christian Culture of Ireland's Apostolic Age* (Notre Dame, Ind.: University of Notre Dame Press, 1993). Translations and commentaries on writings of Patrick plus later documents. Excellent background material.

dePaor, Máire B., P.B.V.M., *Patrick, The Pilgrim Apostle of Ireland: St. Patrick's Confession and Epistola* (San Francisco: Ignatius, 1998). Saint Patrick's *Confessio* and *Epistola* edited and translated with analysis and commentary. Latin text with inclusive language English translation. Fine academic and devotional commentary.

Duffy, Joseph, *Patrick in His Own Words* (Dublin: Veritas, 1996). Text of Patrick's writings in good translation and short commentary.

Holmes, J.M., *The Real Saint Patrick*, (Greenville, S.C.: Ambassador, 1997). Reflections on Saint Patrick in light of the *Confession*.

Howlett, D.R., editor and translator, *The Confession of Saint Patrick*, with introduction by Lawrence S. Cunningham (Ligouri, Mo.: Triumph, 1996). An excellent analytical introduction with an adequate translation.

Joyce, Timothy, O.S.B., *Celtic Christianity: A Sacred Tradition, A Vision of Hope*, (Maryknoll, N.Y.: Orbis Books, 1998). A historical and theological examination of ancient Celtic Christianity and its implications for today.

King, Ursula, *Spirit of Fire: The Life and Vision of Teilhard de Chardin* (Maryknoll, N.Y.: Orbis Books, 1996). Excellent biography and analysis of this extraordinary Jesuit theologian, mystic and scientist.

Mackey, James P., ed., *An Introduction to Celtic Christianity* (Edinburgh: T & T Clark, 1989). A collection of scholarly essays. See especially "The Mission of Saint Patrick" by R.P.C. Hanson and "St. Patrick's Breastplate" by N. D. O'Donoghue.

Mooney, Christopher, *Teilhard de Chardin and the Mystery of Christ* (New York: Harper and Row, 1966). A synthesis of Chardinian thought on the Christ.

O'Donoghue, Noel Dermot, *The Mountain Behind the Mountain: Aspects of the Celtic Tradition* (Edinburgh: T & T Clark, 1993). Ten beautiful reflective essays, including two that relate Chardin to Celtic thought.

Simms, George Otto, *The Real Story of Patrick, Who Became Ireland's Patron Saint* (Dublin: The O'Brien Press, 1993). Reflections on Patrick by the former Church of Ireland Archbishop of Armagh.

Skinner, John, translator and notator, *The Confession of Saint Patrick*, prologue by John O'Donoghue (New York: Image, 1998). Good translation and brief commentary.

Whiteside, Leslie, *The Spirituality of St. Patrick*, (Dublin: Columba Press, 1996). Meditations on Saint Patrick and his life.

Audio

Doherty, Mairead Loughnane, harpist and producer, *The Celtic Christian Era in Poems, Song and Prayer*, with Timothy Joyce, O.S.B., Anam-Chara Records, 33 Curve St., Sherborn, MA 01770. Readings from the *Confession*, Breastplate and other Christian Celtic sources.